RESTORATIVE JUSTICE IN INDIGENOUS COMMUNITIES

Dr. Maxwell Shimba

Printed by Shimba Publishing LLC
Printed in the United States of America

TABLE OF CONTENTS

Introduction v

   1.1 Definition and Principles.. vi

   1.2 Traditional Approaches vs. Restorative Justice xi

   1.3 Indigenous Legal Systems: A Framework for Peace.............. xix

Chapter 01... 1

Indigeneous Legal Traditions 1

Chapter 02 27

The Role of Storytelling in in Indigenous Restorative Practices... 27

   The Role of Storytelling in Indigenous Restorative Practices 35

   The Role of Storytelling in Indigenous Restorative Practices 44

Chapter 03 53

Key Concepts of Restorative Justice in Indigenous Context.......... 53

   Key Concepts of Restorative Justice in Indigenous Contexts........ 61

   Key Concepts of Restorative Justice in Indigenous Contexts........ 70

Chapter 04 81

Case Studies from Indigenous Communities................................. 81

   Case Studies from Indigenous Communities............................ 91

   Case Studies from Indigenous Communities............................ 101

Chapter 05 114

Restorative Justice and Modern Legal System............................ 114

   Restorative Justice and Modern Legal Systems.......................... 124

   Restorative Justice and Modern Legal Systems.......................... 134

Chapter 06..**146**

Restorative Justice in the Context Reconciliation **146**

Restorative Justice in the Context of Reconciliation 157

Restorative Justice in the Context of Reconciliation 168

Chapter 07..**180**

Challenges and Future Directions **180**

Challenges and Future Directions 189

Challenges and Future Directions 198

Chapter 08..**210**

Conclusion..**210**

Chapter 09..**217**

References **217**

INTRODUCTION

Understanding Restorative Justice

Restorative justice is a philosophy and approach to justice that focuses on repairing the harm caused by criminal behavior or conflict, rather than simply punishing the offender. Unlike the retributive justice model, which centers on punishment and the enforcement of legal consequences, restorative justice emphasizes healing, accountability, and the rebuilding of relationships between the victim, the offender, and the broader community. In this sense, it seeks to restore balance and harmony within the social fabric disrupted by the offense.

Restorative justice is rooted in the recognition that crimes and conflicts are not just violations of law but are also deeply social and emotional events that affect individuals and communities. It encourages all parties involved—those who have been harmed, those responsible for the harm, and community members—to come together to understand the impact of the offense and collaboratively determine how to make things right.

In many Indigenous communities, restorative justice aligns with traditional practices of conflict resolution and justice, which have long prioritized communal harmony, healing, and the reintegration of offenders into society. These traditions, often based on principles of interconnectedness, spirituality, and respect for human dignity, offer a rich and enduring foundation for understanding restorative justice.

This section of the book will begin by defining restorative justice and exploring its core principles, contrasting it with traditional Western approaches to justice.

1.1 Definition and Principles

Restorative justice is a process aimed at addressing harm and restoring relationships through dialogue, mutual understanding, and collective decision-making. Its application varies depending on the context, but its essential goal remains constant: to provide a holistic, inclusive approach to justice that promotes healing rather than punishment. The roots of restorative justice can be found in Indigenous legal traditions, but in recent decades, it has been formally recognized and integrated into modern legal systems worldwide.

Definition of Restorative Justice

Restorative justice is typically defined as a process by which those directly affected by an offense—victims, offenders, and community members—are actively involved in resolving the aftermath of the wrongdoing and deciding on the best way to repair harm and address the needs of all parties. It is not limited to criminal justice systems but is also applicable in various contexts, including schools, workplaces, and community disputes.

The process involves:

1. Engagement of all parties affected by the harm. This includes open and inclusive dialogue between the victim, offender, and the community.

2. Acknowledgment of Responsibility by the offender, accepting their role in causing harm.

3. Reparation where the focus is on making amends for the harm caused, which may include apologies, restitution, or actions aimed at repairing relationships.

4. Reintegration into the community, ensuring that the offender is welcomed back as a productive member of society once they have taken responsibility for their actions.

5. Prevention of Recurrence, aiming to reduce the likelihood of future offenses by fostering personal and communal healing.

Core Principles of Restorative Justice

1. Repairing Harm

The central focus of restorative justice is on addressing and repairing the harm caused by an offense. This includes the emotional, physical, and social damage experienced by victims and communities. The process acknowledges that offenses disrupt not only the individuals involved but also the community's peace and balance. Therefore, restorative justice seeks to heal this disruption through meaningful and often symbolic actions that restore equilibrium.

2. Involvement of Stakeholders

Restorative justice processes require the active participation of all stakeholders—victims, offenders, and community members. This differs significantly from the retributive model, where the justice process is typically left in the hands of legal professionals, with limited input from those directly affected by the crime. In restorative justice, dialogue and decision-making occur through collective discussion, emphasizing the voice of the victim and the accountability of the offender.

3. Voluntary Participation

For restorative justice to be effective, the process must be entered into voluntarily by all participants. Coercion undermines the integrity of the restorative process, as genuine accountability and healing require a commitment from the offender to acknowledge their wrongdoing and work toward repairing the harm. Similarly, the victim must willingly participate in seeking resolution, rather than being compelled to confront the offender.

4. Community Involvement and Support

Restorative justice recognizes that offenses often have a ripple effect, impacting not just the direct victims but also the broader community. Therefore, community members are often involved in the process, both as participants in dialogue and as supporters of the outcomes. The community's role is crucial in ensuring that justice is not only done but is also seen to be done, fostering a sense of collective responsibility and healing.

5. Reconciliation and Reintegration

One of the key objectives of restorative justice is the reconciliation of relationships and the reintegration of offenders into their communities. Rather than isolating offenders through punishment, the goal is to help them understand the impact of their actions, take steps to make amends, and reintegrate them as valued community members. This approach helps to prevent the cycle of recidivism and promotes long-term social harmony.

6. Holistic Focus on Healing

Restorative justice is not only about resolving the specific incident of harm but also about addressing broader emotional, social, and sometimes even spiritual wounds. It views justice as a holistic process, where healing is achieved through dialogue, understanding, and collective action. This principle is particularly resonant in Indigenous communities, where justice is seen as inseparable from the health and well-being of the entire community.

7. Restorative Justice as a Process, Not an Outcome

Another distinguishing feature of restorative justice is that it is viewed as an ongoing process rather than a one-time event. The process may begin with a formal meeting or circle, but the ripple effects of dialogue and reparation continue long after. Healing may take time, and the relationships between victims, offenders, and communities evolve as they work toward restoring trust and balance.

Contrasting Restorative Justice with Traditional Retributive Systems

In contrast to restorative justice, traditional Western legal systems are largely based on retributive justice, which focuses on punishment and deterrence. In retributive justice, the state assumes responsibility for addressing offenses, often sidelining the needs of the victim and the role of the community. The primary goal is to determine guilt and administer punishment, often in the form of imprisonment or fines, which is seen as "paying the price" for the crime.

While retributive justice is centered around the punishment of the offender, restorative justice asks more fundamental questions:

- Who has been harmed?

- What are the needs of those involved?

- How can the harm be repaired?

- What can be done to prevent future harm?

The focus shifts from punishment to repair, from retribution to reconciliation, and from isolation to reintegration. This distinction is at the heart of the restorative justice philosophy, offering a more inclusive and healing path forward.

This section lays the groundwork for understanding the principles of restorative justice, which will serve as a foundation for exploring its application within Indigenous communities in later chapters.

1.2 Traditional Approaches vs. Restorative Justice

When discussing justice systems, it is important to recognize the distinction between traditional, often retributive, approaches to justice and the restorative justice framework. Each represents a fundamentally different way of conceptualizing harm, punishment, and the role of the community in conflict resolution.

Traditional Approaches to Justice

Traditional approaches to justice—especially those seen in Western legal systems—are primarily retributive. Retributive justice is rooted in the idea that crime is a violation of the law, and, consequently, it demands punishment. In these systems, the state assumes the role of the primary actor in delivering justice, with the objective of maintaining order, enforcing laws, and deterring future offenses.

Key Characteristics of Traditional Approaches:

1. Focus on Lawbreaking

Traditional justice systems are centered around the violation of state laws. Crime is viewed as an act against the state or legal system, rather than as harm done to individuals or communities. In such systems, the state's interest in maintaining public order takes precedence over addressing the needs of victims or the root causes of the offense.

2. Punishment as a Deterrent

The cornerstone of retributive justice is punishment. Offenders are punished in proportion to their wrongdoing, with the belief that this will serve as a deterrent for both the individual and society at large. This deterrence model assumes that fear of punishment will reduce future criminal behavior.

3. Isolation of the Offender

In traditional justice systems, offenders are often isolated from society through incarceration or other punitive measures. This isolation is viewed as both a form of punishment and a means of protecting society from further harm. However, this model tends to overlook the long-term impact of such isolation, including the social stigma attached to offenders upon their return to the community, and the lack of meaningful rehabilitation during their period of punishment.

4. Minimal Involvement of Victims

In many traditional systems, the role of the victim is limited. Victims may provide testimony in court, but they generally have little say in the outcome or resolution of the case. The primary focus is on determining guilt and meting out punishment, with little attention paid to addressing the emotional, psychological, or material needs of those who were harmed.

5. Formal Legal Procedures

Traditional justice systems rely heavily on formal legal procedures, including adversarial court processes, strict rules of evidence, and legal representation. These processes are often impersonal and can be intimidating or alienating for both victims and offenders. Justice is delivered in a way that is standardized and bureaucratic, often lacking the personal engagement needed for meaningful resolution and healing.

6. Reparation is Rare

Traditional justice models rarely emphasize the need for offenders to make reparations to their victims or the community. Financial penalties or other forms of restitution are sometimes included in sentencing, but they are often insufficient to repair the deeper emotional or social harm caused by the offense.

Restorative Justice: A Contrast

In contrast to traditional retributive justice, restorative justice focuses on healing the harm caused by crime, fostering dialogue between victims, offenders, and the community. It emphasizes accountability, making amends, and reintegration, rather than punishment and exclusion.

Key Characteristics of Restorative Justice:

1. Focus on Harm and Relationships

Restorative justice views crime not just as a violation of the law but as harm done to people and relationships. It seeks to repair the damage caused by the offense, acknowledging that crime disrupts the social fabric and causes emotional, psychological, and sometimes physical harm to individuals and communities.

2. Accountability and Responsibility

In restorative justice, accountability is not synonymous with punishment. Instead, offenders are encouraged to take responsibility for their actions by acknowledging the harm they have caused and participating in a process that seeks to repair that harm. This approach views accountability as a constructive process rather than a punitive one.

3. Involvement of All Parties

One of the most distinguishing features of restorative justice is its inclusive nature. It brings together victims, offenders, and community members to participate in dialogue, aiming to reach a mutually agreed-upon resolution. This participation ensures that the voices of those most affected by the offense are heard and that the resolution addresses their needs.

4. Reparation and Healing

Unlike traditional approaches that focus on punishment, restorative justice prioritizes reparation. Offenders are expected to make amends for the harm they have caused, which may involve apologies, restitution, or community service. The goal is to heal the damage done to individuals, relationships, and communities, fostering reconciliation and closure.

5. Community-Centered Approach

Restorative justice sees crime as a disruption of the community's peace and harmony, not just a violation of laws. Therefore, the community plays an integral role in the justice process. In many Indigenous cultures, community members actively participate in the resolution process, whether through restorative circles, peacemaking sessions, or other traditional practices that emphasize collective well-being.

6. Reintegration of Offenders

Instead of isolating offenders from society, restorative justice seeks to reintegrate them into the community once they have taken responsibility for their actions and made amends. This approach reduces recidivism by focusing on rehabilitation and social reintegration, rather than perpetuating a cycle of punishment and exclusion.

7. Flexibility and Informality

Unlike the rigid procedures of traditional legal systems, restorative justice is flexible and adaptable to the needs of the people involved. The process is often informal, conducted in community spaces rather than courtrooms, and tailored to the cultural and social context of the community. This flexibility allows for a more personal and meaningful resolution to the conflict.

Case Study: Traditional vs. Restorative Justice in Indigenous Communities

Indigenous communities often embody restorative justice principles in their traditional conflict resolution methods. For instance, in many First Nations and Native American communities, justice is seen as a means of restoring balance and harmony within the community, rather than as a system for punishing wrongdoers.

Example: Circle Sentencing

Circle sentencing, practiced by many Indigenous communities in Canada, is a restorative justice practice that brings together the victim, offender, and community members in a circle to discuss the impact of the offense and determine a collective resolution. In contrast to the adversarial nature of Western court systems, where the state takes center stage, circle sentencing prioritizes the community's role in achieving justice and healing. It involves dialogue, consensus-building, and a shared responsibility for the outcome.

Traditional Western approaches would likely incarcerate the offender, isolating them from their community and providing little opportunity for them to make amends. In a circle sentencing process, however, the focus is on reparation and reintegration, ensuring that the offender remains connected to their community and has a path to restoration.

Key Differences Between Traditional and Restorative Justice

Aspect	Traditional Justice	Restorative Justice
Focus	Crime as a violation of the law	Crime as harm to people and relationships

Goal	Punishment and deterrence	Reparation, healing, and reconciliation
Offender's Role	Offender is punished and often isolated from the community	Offender takes responsibility and makes amends
Victim's Role	Minimal involvement; often passive	Active participant in the process
Community's Role	Largely absent; the state is the primary actor	Integral to the process; justice is seen as a collective responsibility
Outcome	Punitive measures (e.g., imprisonment, fines)	Restitution, reconciliation, reintegration

Conclusion: Moving Toward Restorative Justice

While traditional justice systems have long dominated legal frameworks in many parts of the world, the restorative justice model offers an alternative that emphasizes healing, accountability, and community involvement. This approach aligns closely with the values of many Indigenous cultures, which have long practiced justice in a way that prioritizes collective well-being and the restoration of social harmony.

As modern legal systems begin to recognize the value of restorative justice, particularly in addressing the unique needs of Indigenous communities, there is an increasing movement toward integrating these principles into broader frameworks. This chapter has highlighted the fundamental differences between traditional and restorative justice, setting the stage for a deeper exploration of how Indigenous communities practice restorative justice and how these practices can inform and improve contemporary justice systems.

1.3 Indigenous Legal Systems: A Framework for Peace

Indigenous legal systems are deeply rooted in the social, cultural, and spiritual traditions of Indigenous communities. These systems are designed not only to address wrongdoing but also to maintain harmony, balance, and peace within the community. They are holistic in nature, viewing justice as inseparable from the health and well-being of individuals, families, and the larger social fabric.

Unlike Western legal frameworks, which are often adversarial and focused on punitive outcomes, Indigenous legal systems prioritize restorative practices. Their emphasis is on the collective responsibility of the community, repairing harm, and ensuring that all members of the community, including both victims and offenders, are restored to a state of balance.

Key Characteristics of Indigenous Legal Systems

1. Holistic Approach to Justice

Indigenous legal systems are built on the principle that justice must address not only the immediate harm caused by a conflict or crime but also the broader impact on the community's peace and well-being. They recognize the interconnectedness of individuals, families, and the environment, and thus, any disruption to this interconnectedness must be addressed through a process that restores harmony at all levels. Healing is central to this process, both for the individual and the community.

Indigenous approaches to justice consider physical, emotional, spiritual, and social dimensions. Justice is not merely about adjudicating right and wrong but about creating conditions for long-term peace and healing. This holistic view contrasts sharply with the compartmentalized nature of many Western legal systems, where legal, psychological, and social issues are often addressed separately.

2. Emphasis on Community Responsibility

In Indigenous communities, justice is seen as a collective responsibility. The entire community is involved in addressing wrongdoing and resolving conflicts. This involvement can take many forms, such as peacemaking circles, elders' councils, or community meetings, where all affected parties participate in dialogue and decision-making.

This communal approach stems from the belief that crime or conflict harms not just the individuals involved but the entire community. Therefore, it is the community's responsibility to restore peace and balance. This differs from Western legal systems, where the state typically takes over the role of adjudicator and enforcer, often sidelining the role of community members.

3. Reintegration and Healing

Indigenous legal systems prioritize the reintegration of offenders into the community. Rather than seeking to punish or isolate those who have caused harm, Indigenous justice processes focus on ensuring that offenders take responsibility for their actions and make amends to those affected. Once the harm is repaired, the offender is welcomed back into the community as a valued member.

This focus on reintegration is particularly important in maintaining social cohesion within close-knit Indigenous communities. The aim is not to alienate or exclude individuals, but to ensure that they remain part of the social and cultural fabric of the community after they have taken steps to address the harm they caused. Offenders are given the opportunity to heal alongside the victims, and the entire community benefits from this approach to justice.

4. The Role of Elders

Elders hold a special place in Indigenous legal systems. As carriers of wisdom, tradition, and spiritual guidance, elders often play a central role in resolving disputes and facilitating justice processes. Their involvement is crucial to the functioning of Indigenous justice, as they provide cultural continuity and a moral compass for the community.

Elders serve as mediators, peacemakers, and advisors in many Indigenous legal systems. Their knowledge of cultural norms, values, and historical context allows them to guide the community through the process of resolving conflicts in ways that honor tradition and ensure fairness. The respect afforded to elders in Indigenous communities is a vital component of maintaining social order and harmony.

5. Spiritual and Cultural Dimensions of Justice

Justice in Indigenous communities is often intertwined with spiritual and cultural beliefs. Many Indigenous traditions view wrongdoing as a spiritual imbalance or a disruption of the harmony between individuals, families, and the natural world. As a result, justice processes often incorporate spiritual practices, such as prayer, ceremony, or ritual, to help restore balance and promote healing.

This spiritual dimension of justice contrasts with the secular nature of many Western legal systems, where spiritual or cultural considerations are often marginalized or excluded from legal proceedings. In Indigenous communities, justice cannot be separated from spirituality, as it is an integral part of the process of healing and reconciliation.

Restorative Practices in Indigenous Legal Systems

Restorative justice is often seen as a modern approach to justice reform, but it is, in many ways, a reflection of the time-honored practices found in Indigenous legal systems. Many Indigenous communities have long practiced forms of restorative justice that prioritize healing, community involvement, and accountability. These practices are built on the core belief that justice should restore harmony, rather than simply punish wrongdoing.

1. Peacemaking Circles

A key practice in many Indigenous legal systems is the use of peacemaking circles, where members of the community gather in a circle to discuss and resolve conflicts. In these circles, everyone affected by the wrongdoing—victims, offenders, family members, and community representatives—has an opportunity to speak and contribute to the resolution. The process is inclusive and emphasizes dialogue, understanding, and consensus-building.

The circle symbolizes equality and interconnectedness, with each participant holding an equal voice in the discussion. The goal is not to assign blame or deliver punishment, but to restore relationships and repair the harm done to the community. The process encourages open communication, empathy, and shared responsibility for the outcome.

2. Elders' Councils and Healing Circles

In many Indigenous communities, elders' councils or healing circles are used to address conflict and wrongdoing. Elders guide the discussion, using their wisdom to mediate the situation and offer culturally appropriate solutions. The focus is on healing, reconciliation, and restoring harmony within the community.

Healing circles, in particular, emphasize the importance of emotional and spiritual well-being in the justice process. Offenders are given the opportunity to express remorse, and victims can voice their pain in a supportive environment. The collective goal is to reach a resolution that allows both parties to heal and move forward in peace.

3. Restitution and Reconciliation

Restitution—making amends for the harm caused— is a central element of Indigenous justice systems. Offenders are expected to take concrete actions to repair the damage they have done, whether through apologies, compensation, or community service. The aim is to ensure that the harm is acknowledged and addressed in a meaningful way.

Reconciliation is the ultimate goal of Indigenous justice systems. It is not enough for an offender to be punished; the community seeks to repair the relationship between the victim, the offender, and the broader community. Once restitution has been made, efforts are focused on reintegrating the offender into the community and restoring peace and balance.

Colonization and the Suppression of Indigenous Legal Systems

The imposition of colonial legal systems significantly disrupted Indigenous justice practices. As colonial powers expanded, Indigenous legal systems were often suppressed or marginalized, with Western-style courts and punitive measures replacing traditional forms of justice. This disruption had long-lasting effects on Indigenous communities, contributing to the breakdown of social cohesion and the erosion of cultural identity.

Colonial legal systems often viewed Indigenous practices as primitive or inferior, failing to recognize the value of their restorative and holistic approaches to justice. As a result, Indigenous peoples were forced to navigate legal systems that were alien to their cultural values and ways of life. The emphasis on punishment and retribution in colonial legal systems often clashed with Indigenous traditions of healing and reconciliation.

In recent decades, there has been a resurgence of interest in Indigenous legal traditions and their potential to offer alternatives to punitive justice systems. Many Indigenous communities are actively reviving their justice practices, working to integrate them into contemporary legal frameworks and reclaiming their authority to resolve conflicts in ways that align with their cultural values.

Conclusion: A Framework for Peace

Indigenous legal systems offer a powerful framework for achieving peace and harmony within communities. By prioritizing healing, accountability, and the restoration of relationships, these systems provide an alternative to the adversarial, punitive approach of many Western legal systems. The emphasis on community involvement, reintegration, and spiritual well-being makes Indigenous legal systems uniquely suited to fostering long-term peace.

As we explore restorative justice in Indigenous contexts, it is important to recognize the enduring value of these legal traditions. They provide a blueprint for addressing conflict in a way that is compassionate, inclusive, and culturally grounded. By learning from and honoring these traditions, we can work toward a justice system that promotes healing, reconciliation, and lasting peace for all.

xxvii

DR. MAXWELL SHIMBA

CHAPTER 01

INDIGENEOUS LEGAL TRADITIONS

1.1 Indigenous Communities and Justice: A Historical Perspective

Indigenous communities across the globe have long-standing legal traditions that precede the introduction of Western legal systems. These traditions, deeply rooted in cultural, spiritual, and social practices, have guided Indigenous peoples in maintaining peace, resolving conflicts, and ensuring the well-being of their communities for centuries. Understanding these Indigenous legal traditions requires a historical perspective that acknowledges their complexity, adaptability, and resilience, despite the challenges posed by colonization and the imposition of foreign legal frameworks.

Pre-Colonial Justice Systems

Before the arrival of European colonizers, Indigenous communities in regions such as North America, Australia, New Zealand, and Africa operated under their own legal systems, often referred to as customary law. These systems were based on shared values of kinship, reciprocity, respect for the natural world, and a deep understanding of the interconnectedness of all community members. Justice was not merely about adjudicating disputes but about maintaining balance and harmony in the community.

Key Features of Pre-Colonial Indigenous Justice Systems:

1. Oral Tradition and Knowledge Transmission

Indigenous legal systems were largely oral, with laws, customs, and values passed down through generations by storytelling, ceremonies, and the guidance of elders. These oral traditions provided a flexible, dynamic means of transmitting legal knowledge, ensuring that laws were adaptable to the evolving needs of the community. Legal knowledge was often embedded in spiritual teachings, stories of creation, and cultural narratives that emphasized collective responsibility and respect for life.

2. Kinship and Collective Responsibility

Justice in Indigenous communities was often rooted in the concept of kinship. The well-being of the individual was intimately connected to the well-being of the family, clan, and community. Therefore, resolving disputes or addressing harm was seen as a collective responsibility. When a person committed an offense, it was not only their individual actions that were examined, but the impact on the wider community. The offender's family often played a role in making amends and restoring balance.

3. Restorative Justice Practices

Many Indigenous communities practiced forms of justice that closely align with what we now call restorative justice. The primary goal was to restore harmony within the community rather than to punish the offender. Methods included negotiation, mediation, and reconciliation processes that involved victims, offenders, and community members. The focus was on repairing harm, mending relationships, and reintegrating offenders back into the community once amends had been made.

4. The Role of Elders and Spiritual Leaders

Elders and spiritual leaders played a crucial role in Indigenous justice systems. As the keepers of cultural and legal knowledge, elders were often called upon to mediate conflicts, offer guidance, and ensure that justice processes were aligned with the community's spiritual and cultural values. Their authority was not based on formal laws or institutions but on their deep wisdom, experience, and the trust placed in them by the community.

5. Community-Based Decision Making

Indigenous justice was inherently communal. Decisions about how to address wrongdoing were often made through consensus, with the participation of those directly involved as well as other community members. This collective decision-making process ensured that the needs of all parties—victims, offenders, and the broader community—were taken into account. The aim was not only to resolve the immediate conflict but to strengthen social bonds and prevent future harm.

Impact of Colonization on Indigenous Legal Systems

The arrival of European colonizers brought profound disruption to Indigenous legal systems. Colonial governments imposed their own legal frameworks, often disregarding or undermining the legal traditions of Indigenous peoples. Indigenous laws and customs were labeled as primitive or inferior, and colonizers sought to replace them with Western legal systems based on European notions of justice, property, and governance.

1. Displacement of Indigenous Legal Authority

One of the most significant impacts of colonization was the displacement of Indigenous legal authority. Colonial governments introduced their own courts, laws, and systems of governance, often through violence and coercion. Indigenous leaders, elders, and spiritual figures who had traditionally served as mediators of justice were marginalized, and their authority was eroded. This led to a breakdown in Indigenous legal systems, as communities were forced to navigate foreign legal processes that did not align with their cultural values or ways of life.

2. Criminalization of Indigenous Practices

Many aspects of Indigenous culture and legal practices were criminalized under colonial rule. Ceremonial practices, religious rituals, and traditional forms of conflict resolution were banned or restricted. In some cases, Indigenous people were punished for adhering to their customs, and Indigenous legal systems were dismissed as barbaric or uncivilized. For example, in Canada and the United States, Indigenous ceremonies such as the potlatch and the Sun Dance were banned, leading to the suppression of spiritual and legal traditions that were integral to Indigenous communities.

3. Forced Assimilation and Legal Displacement

The imposition of colonial legal systems was often accompanied by policies of forced assimilation. Indigenous peoples were pressured to abandon their languages, spiritual beliefs, and customs in favor of adopting European ways of life. Legal systems were a key part of this assimilation process. Indigenous children were removed from their families and placed in residential or boarding schools, where they were taught to reject their cultural identity. Indigenous governance structures were replaced with colonial models of governance, further undermining Indigenous legal traditions.

4. Resistance and Adaptation

Despite the overwhelming pressure to assimilate, Indigenous communities have resisted the complete erasure of their legal systems. Many Indigenous peoples found ways to preserve their legal traditions, sometimes in secret, and adapted them to survive in the face of colonial oppression. Elders continued to pass down legal knowledge orally, and community-based justice practices were maintained even when they were forced underground. In recent decades, there has been a resurgence of interest in reviving and strengthening Indigenous legal systems, both within Indigenous communities and in collaboration with national legal systems.

Revival and Resurgence of Indigenous Legal Traditions

In recent years, Indigenous communities have actively sought to reclaim and revitalize their legal traditions. This resurgence is part of a broader movement toward decolonization, self-determination, and the recognition of Indigenous rights. As Indigenous peoples work to heal from the historical trauma of colonization, their legal systems are being recognized as vital to maintaining cultural identity and sovereignty.

1. Reassertion of Sovereignty

The revival of Indigenous legal traditions is closely tied to the broader movement for Indigenous sovereignty. Across the world, Indigenous peoples are reasserting their right to govern themselves and maintain their own legal systems. In many cases, Indigenous communities are working to integrate their traditional justice practices into national legal frameworks, seeking recognition of their laws alongside state and federal systems. This resurgence of legal traditions is not only about reclaiming the past but also about creating a future in which Indigenous peoples have the authority to manage their own affairs and resolve conflicts in ways that align with their values.

2. Restorative Justice and Indigenous Legal Practices

The growing recognition of restorative justice as an alternative to punitive legal systems has led to renewed interest in Indigenous legal practices. Many modern restorative justice programs are inspired by Indigenous traditions of conflict resolution and community-based justice. Practices such as circle sentencing, peacemaking, and healing circles have been adapted into contemporary legal systems, providing models for addressing harm that prioritize healing, accountability, and community involvement. These practices are rooted in Indigenous worldviews that emphasize the importance of relationships, reciprocity, and collective well-being.

3. Legal Recognition and Land Claims

In some countries, Indigenous legal systems have gained recognition within national and international legal frameworks. For example, the United Nations Declaration on the Rights of Indigenous Peoples (UNDRIP) recognizes the right of Indigenous peoples to maintain their own legal institutions and resolve disputes according to their customs. Additionally, Indigenous land claims and treaty negotiations have provided opportunities for Indigenous peoples to assert their legal traditions in defense of their rights to land, resources, and self-determination.

Conclusion: A Legacy of Justice

Indigenous legal systems have endured centuries of colonization, repression, and marginalization, yet they remain resilient and vibrant in many communities today. These systems offer a powerful model of justice that prioritizes healing, relationships, and community well-being over punishment and retribution. As Indigenous peoples continue to reclaim their legal traditions, they provide valuable lessons for addressing the limitations of Western legal systems and creating more just, inclusive societies.

This historical perspective on Indigenous communities and justice sets the stage for a deeper exploration of the key principles, practices, and challenges that define Indigenous legal traditions in the modern era. These traditions are not relics of the past but living systems of law that continue to evolve and adapt, offering a framework for peace and reconciliation in a world that often struggles to find meaningful solutions to conflict and harm.

1.2 Colonization and Legal Systems

Colonization dramatically transformed the legal landscapes of Indigenous communities around the world. As European powers expanded their territories across North America, South America, Africa, Australia, and parts of Asia, they imposed their own legal systems on Indigenous peoples, often with devastating effects. The colonizers sought to replace Indigenous governance structures and justice practices with European legal frameworks, which were based on principles of property ownership, individualism, and retribution. This process of legal imposition was a central part of the broader colonial strategy to subjugate and assimilate

Indigenous peoples, undermining their cultures, traditions, and sovereignty.

The Legal Imposition of Colonial Rule

Colonial powers introduced new legal systems that were fundamentally at odds with the collective, restorative, and relationship-based approaches to justice practiced by many Indigenous communities. These colonial legal systems were designed to enforce the laws and norms of the colonizers, facilitate land appropriation, and regulate relations between Indigenous peoples and settlers. The introduction of Western legal systems had several immediate and long-lasting effects on Indigenous communities, including the erosion of traditional authority structures, the criminalization of Indigenous practices, and the alienation of Indigenous peoples from their lands and resources.

Key Characteristics of Colonial Legal Systems:

1. Imposition of European Legal Frameworks

Colonial powers imposed European legal frameworks on Indigenous populations without regard for their existing legal systems or governance structures. These frameworks were based on principles of individual rights, private property, and punitive justice, which clashed with the collective, land-based, and restorative traditions of many Indigenous communities. European laws were enforced through courts, police forces, and other colonial institutions, which often viewed Indigenous practices as inferior or uncivilized.

2. Focus on Property and Resource Control

One of the primary objectives of colonial legal systems was to facilitate the control and extraction of land and resources. Indigenous peoples were often dispossessed of their lands through treaties, legal doctrines like terra nullius (the idea that land not occupied by Europeans was legally "empty"), or outright force. Colonial legal systems justified the appropriation of Indigenous lands for the benefit of settlers and colonial governments, ignoring Indigenous concepts of communal land stewardship and sovereignty.

3. Criminalization of Indigenous Practices

Many Indigenous cultural, spiritual, and legal practices were outlawed under colonial rule. Ceremonies, governance structures, and conflict resolution methods that had been central to Indigenous life for centuries were often labeled as criminal or primitive. In North America, for example, practices like the Potlatch (among Pacific Northwest Indigenous peoples) and the Sun Dance (among Plains Indigenous peoples) were banned, and violators faced imprisonment or other punishments. These bans were part of a broader effort to assimilate Indigenous peoples into Western ways of life and to undermine their legal autonomy.

4. Displacement of Indigenous Leadership

Colonial authorities often sought to replace or co-opt Indigenous leadership structures. Traditional leaders, such as chiefs or elders, who had maintained authority within their communities, were marginalized or stripped of their power. In some cases, colonial governments appointed Indigenous leaders who were seen as more compliant or aligned with colonial interests, leading to internal divisions within Indigenous communities. The displacement of traditional leaders further weakened Indigenous legal systems and made it difficult for communities to maintain their cultural practices and self-governance.

5. Introduction of Punitive Justice

Colonial legal systems were largely punitive, focusing on punishing offenders rather than repairing harm or restoring relationships. In contrast, many Indigenous legal systems emphasized healing, reconciliation, and restoring balance within the community. The introduction of prisons, courts, and other colonial institutions created a justice system that was adversarial and focused on punishment, often leading to the incarceration and marginalization of Indigenous peoples. This punitive approach conflicted with the restorative principles that had guided Indigenous justice for generations.

Doctrines and Legal Tools Used to Dispossess Indigenous Peoples

Colonial powers developed a range of legal doctrines and tools to justify the dispossession of Indigenous peoples and the imposition of colonial rule. These legal frameworks were often cloaked in the language of law and justice, but their primary purpose was to legitimize the seizure of land, resources, and political power.

1. Doctrine of Discovery

The Doctrine of Discovery was a key legal principle that justified European colonization of lands inhabited by Indigenous peoples. This doctrine, rooted in papal bulls issued by the Catholic Church in the 15th century, declared that any land not inhabited by Christians could be claimed by Christian rulers. It provided the legal foundation for European powers to claim sovereignty over lands in the Americas, Africa, and Asia, regardless of the presence of Indigenous populations.

The Doctrine of Discovery treated Indigenous peoples as occupants of the land, but not as rightful owners with legal title. This doctrine was later enshrined in legal decisions, such as the U.S. Supreme Court case Johnson v. M'Intosh (1823), which held that Indigenous peoples had only a right of occupancy, while ultimate title to the land rested with European sovereigns or their successors. This legal reasoning was used to justify the widespread seizure of Indigenous lands by European settlers and governments.

2. Terra Nullius

The legal concept of terra nullius, meaning "land belonging to no one," was another tool used by colonial powers to claim sovereignty over Indigenous lands. European colonizers often declared that the lands they encountered were legally "empty" because they were not being used in ways that Europeans recognized as legitimate, such as farming or permanent settlement. This doctrine ignored Indigenous peoples' long-standing presence on the land, their deep spiritual connections to the land, and their sustainable land management practices.

In Australia, for example, the British government declared the continent to be terra nullius upon colonization in 1788, despite the presence of Indigenous peoples who had lived there for tens of thousands of years. It was not until the Mabo case in 1992 that the Australian legal system formally rejected the concept of terra nullius and recognized Indigenous land rights.

3. Treaties and Legal Manipulation

In many parts of the world, colonial powers entered into treaties with Indigenous peoples, often presenting them as agreements for mutual benefit. However, these treaties were frequently negotiated under duress, with Indigenous leaders having little understanding of European legal concepts, and they were often violated or ignored by colonial governments.

In North America, for example, treaties between Indigenous nations and colonial governments were supposed to establish peaceful relations and define land rights. However, these treaties were frequently broken as settlers and governments encroached on Indigenous lands. Legal manipulation, including the use of ambiguous language and the failure to honor treaty commitments, was a common tactic used to dispossess Indigenous peoples of their lands and resources.

4. The Indian Act and Legal Control

In Canada, the Indian Act of 1876 exemplifies how colonial governments used legal systems to control Indigenous populations and undermine their autonomy. The Indian Act consolidated various laws relating to Indigenous peoples and gave the Canadian government sweeping authority over nearly every aspect of Indigenous life, from governance structures to land use and cultural practices. The Act imposed a legal framework that treated Indigenous peoples as wards of the state, restricting their rights and freedoms.

One of the most damaging aspects of the Indian Act was its role in the residential school system, which forcibly removed Indigenous children from their families and communities to assimilate them into Western culture. The legal control exerted by the Indian Act and similar legislation in other countries contributed to the erosion of Indigenous legal traditions and cultural practices.

Resistance to Colonial Legal Systems

Despite the overwhelming pressure to conform to colonial legal systems, Indigenous communities have consistently resisted the imposition of foreign laws. Throughout history, Indigenous peoples have fought to maintain their legal traditions, governance structures, and land rights, even in the face of violence, repression, and legal manipulation.

1. Legal Challenges and Advocacy

Indigenous peoples have used both traditional and colonial legal systems to challenge the legitimacy of colonial laws and assert their rights. In many countries, Indigenous leaders have taken their cases to court, demanding recognition of their land rights, treaty obligations, and cultural practices. Legal victories, such as the Mabo case in Australia and the recognition of land rights for the Māori in New Zealand, demonstrate the resilience and adaptability of Indigenous legal systems in the face of colonial domination.

2. Cultural and Spiritual Survival

Even when Indigenous legal practices were banned or suppressed, many communities continued to practice their traditions in secret or adapted them to new circumstances. Elders and spiritual leaders played a crucial role in preserving legal knowledge and passing it down to future generations. Ceremonies, storytelling, and oral traditions became essential tools for maintaining cultural continuity and resisting the erasure of Indigenous legal systems.

3. Revitalization of Indigenous Legal Systems

In recent decades, there has been a resurgence of interest in revitalizing Indigenous legal systems. Many Indigenous communities are reclaiming their legal traditions, incorporating them into modern governance structures, and asserting their right to self-determination. This revitalization is often part of broader movements for decolonization, land reclamation, and cultural revitalization.

Conclusion: The Legacy of Colonization on Indigenous Legal Systems

Colonization profoundly disrupted Indigenous legal systems, replacing restorative and community-based justice with punitive, property-focused legal frameworks. However, Indigenous peoples have resisted the imposition of these colonial systems and continue to fight for the recognition of their legal traditions, governance structures, and sovereignty.

As we move into the next chapters, we will explore how Indigenous legal systems have survived, adapted, and thrived despite colonization. The resilience of these systems offers valuable lessons for understanding justice in ways that are holistic, community-centered, and rooted in the principles of healing and reconciliation.

1.3 Indigenous Legal Systems: A Framework for Peace

Indigenous legal systems have long served as foundational pillars for maintaining peace, harmony, and order within Indigenous communities. These systems are deeply intertwined with the cultural, spiritual, and social fabric of Indigenous life, reflecting values of reciprocity, community responsibility, and respect for the natural world. Unlike many Western legal frameworks, which often prioritize punishment and retribution, Indigenous legal systems emphasize healing, reconciliation, and the restoration of balance. They offer an alternative vision of justice—one that seeks not only to address wrongdoing but also to create the conditions necessary for long-term peace and social cohesion.

Key Features of Indigenous Legal Systems

Indigenous legal systems are diverse and vary significantly across different cultures and regions. However, several key principles and practices are common to many Indigenous justice traditions. These systems emphasize the interconnectedness of individuals, families, and communities and prioritize collective well-being over individual punishment.

1. Holistic Approach to Justice

Indigenous legal systems take a holistic approach to justice, recognizing that harm affects not only the individual who has been wronged but also the community as a whole. Justice is seen as a process that involves healing the physical, emotional, spiritual, and social wounds caused by wrongdoing. The aim is not simply to punish the offender but to restore harmony and balance in the relationships that have been disrupted.

This holistic approach is rooted in the belief that all aspects of life—human relationships, spiritual well-being, and connection to the land—are interconnected. Therefore, when harm occurs, it creates an imbalance that must be addressed through a comprehensive process of healing. This contrasts sharply with the compartmentalized nature of many Western legal systems, where legal, social, and psychological issues are often treated separately.

2. Community Involvement and Collective Responsibility

In Indigenous legal systems, justice is not seen as the responsibility of a distant authority or institution, but as a collective process that involves the entire community. Communities play an active role in resolving conflicts, providing support to victims, holding offenders accountable, and facilitating reconciliation. This involvement reflects the belief that the well-being of individuals is inseparable from the well-being of the community as a whole.

Collective responsibility is a core principle in Indigenous justice. When an individual causes harm, their actions are viewed as affecting not only the victim but the entire community. As a result, it is the community's responsibility to help repair the damage and ensure that the offender is held accountable in a way that promotes healing. This collective process contrasts with Western legal systems, where responsibility for justice is often delegated to state institutions, such as courts and law enforcement.

3. Restorative Justice and Reconciliation

At the heart of many Indigenous legal systems is the concept of restorative justice, a process that seeks to repair the harm caused by wrongdoing and restore relationships between the victim, the offender, and the community. Unlike retributive justice, which focuses on punishment, restorative justice aims to heal the wounds caused by conflict and ensure that both the victim and the offender can move forward in peace.

In a restorative justice process, the offender is encouraged to take responsibility for their actions, acknowledge the harm they have caused, and make amends to the victim and the community. This process often involves direct dialogue between the victim and the offender, mediated by community members or elders. The goal is not only to provide closure for the victim but also to reintegrate the offender into the community in a way that promotes healing and prevents future harm.

4. The Role of Elders and Traditional Leaders

Elders and traditional leaders hold a central place in Indigenous legal systems. They are the keepers of cultural and spiritual knowledge, and they play a key role in mediating disputes and guiding the justice process. Elders are often seen as impartial and wise figures who can facilitate dialogue, offer guidance, and ensure that justice is administered in accordance with cultural values and traditions.

In many Indigenous communities, the involvement of elders is crucial to the legitimacy of the justice process. Their authority is not derived from formal legal institutions but from their deep connection to the community and their knowledge of customary law. Elders often act as mediators in restorative justice processes, helping to bring about reconciliation and ensure that the offender is reintegrated into the community in a respectful and meaningful way.

5. Spiritual and Cultural Dimensions of Justice

Indigenous legal systems are deeply spiritual, recognizing that justice is not only a matter of resolving disputes but also of restoring balance in the broader spiritual and cultural context of the community. Many Indigenous justice processes incorporate spiritual practices, such as ceremonies, prayers, or rituals, as part of the healing process. These practices help to reconnect individuals to their cultural and spiritual roots, providing a sense of closure and peace.

For many Indigenous peoples, justice cannot be separated from spiritual well-being. Wrongdoing is often seen as a disturbance to the natural order, and justice processes aim to restore harmony not only between individuals but also between the community and the spiritual world. This spiritual dimension of justice is often absent in Western legal systems, where secular laws and institutions dominate.

Examples of Indigenous Legal Systems as Frameworks for Peace

Several Indigenous legal systems provide powerful examples of how traditional practices can promote peace and reconciliation within communities. These systems offer alternative models of justice that prioritize healing, community involvement, and the reintegration of offenders.

1. Navajo Peacemaking (North America)

The Navajo Nation in the southwestern United States has long practiced peacemaking, a traditional form of conflict resolution that seeks to restore harmony within the community. Peacemaking involves the participation of all parties affected by a conflict, including victims, offenders, and community members, in a dialogue facilitated by a respected peacemaker, often an elder.

Peacemaking emphasizes the restoration of relationships and the healing of emotional and spiritual wounds. Offenders are encouraged to take responsibility for their actions and make amends, while victims are given the opportunity to express their feelings and receive support from the community. The process is designed to promote reconciliation, rather than punishment, and to reintegrate the offender into the community.

2. Circle Sentencing (Canada)

Circle sentencing, used in many First Nations communities in Canada, is a form of restorative justice that brings together the victim, the offender, their families, and community members in a sentencing circle. The circle format emphasizes equality and open dialogue, with all participants having an equal voice in determining the appropriate resolution to the conflict.

The goal of circle sentencing is to address the underlying causes of the offense, repair the harm caused, and ensure that the offender takes responsibility for their actions. The process is based on the principles of restorative justice and seeks to restore balance and harmony within the community. Circle sentencing has been adapted into the Canadian legal system and is used as an alternative to traditional court sentencing for certain cases.

3. Māori Justice Practices (New Zealand)

The Māori people of New Zealand have a long tradition of restorative justice known as whakawhanaungatanga, which emphasizes the importance of relationships and community involvement in resolving disputes. Māori justice practices are based on the principle that harm disrupts the balance within the whānau (family) and the wider community, and that justice must restore that balance.

Māori justice practices often involve hui (meetings), where the offender, the victim, and their families come together to discuss the harm caused and determine a way forward. The focus is on repairing relationships and ensuring that the offender is held accountable in a way that promotes healing and reconciliation. Māori justice practices have influenced New Zealand's modern restorative justice system, which is now integrated into the formal legal framework.

Indigenous Legal Systems and Contemporary Challenges

While Indigenous legal systems offer valuable frameworks for peace and justice, they also face significant challenges in the modern world. Colonization, urbanization, and the imposition of Western legal systems have disrupted traditional justice practices in many Indigenous communities. Additionally, efforts to integrate Indigenous justice practices into formal legal systems often encounter resistance from legal institutions that are unfamiliar with or skeptical of restorative justice.

However, many Indigenous communities are actively working to revitalize their legal traditions and assert their right to self-determination. In doing so, they are not only preserving their cultural heritage but also providing alternative models of justice that can serve as valuable examples for broader efforts to reform legal systems around the world.

Conclusion: A Framework for Peace

Indigenous legal systems offer a powerful framework for achieving peace within communities by prioritizing healing, reconciliation, and the restoration of relationships. These systems provide an alternative to punitive models of justice, focusing instead on collective responsibility, community involvement, and spiritual well-being. As Indigenous communities continue to reclaim and revitalize their legal traditions, they offer valuable lessons for creating more just, compassionate, and peaceful societies.

By exploring these systems, we can gain insight into how justice can be a process of healing rather than punishment—one that fosters long-term peace and strengthens the social fabric of communities. In a world that often seeks retribution, Indigenous legal systems remind us that true justice is about restoring balance, mending relationships, and creating the conditions for lasting peace.

CHAPTER 02

THE ROLE OF STORYTELLING IN IN INDIGENOUS RESTORATIVE PRACTICES

2.1 Oral Traditions and Knowledge Sharing

In Indigenous cultures around the world, storytelling and oral traditions are not merely forms of entertainment but serve as essential means of transmitting knowledge, preserving history, and maintaining social order. These oral traditions form the foundation of Indigenous legal systems, social norms, and restorative practices, playing a crucial role in how justice is understood and implemented. Through stories, lessons about morality, responsibility, and the consequences of actions are passed down through generations, providing guidance for conflict resolution and maintaining harmony within communities.

Storytelling is a powerful tool for teaching restorative justice principles because it engages listeners on an emotional and intellectual level. It allows community members to reflect on shared values, cultural practices, and the importance of relationships, fostering a sense of collective responsibility. In many Indigenous communities, justice is not only about addressing wrongs but also about reinforcing the social and moral fabric of the community. Stories are key to this process, as they encapsulate the values, customs, and practices that help individuals and communities navigate conflicts, resolve disputes, and heal from harm.

The Importance of Oral Traditions in Indigenous Communities

Oral traditions have been central to Indigenous cultures for thousands of years. Long before the advent of written languages, Indigenous peoples developed sophisticated systems of communication and knowledge transmission through spoken word, songs, dances, and rituals. These oral traditions were, and continue to be, essential for maintaining a sense of identity, preserving historical knowledge, and ensuring the survival of cultural practices.

1. Transmission of Cultural Values and Social Norms

Stories in Indigenous communities often serve as vehicles for conveying the values and principles that guide everyday life. Through oral traditions, elders and community leaders share knowledge about the roles and responsibilities of individuals within the community, the importance of kinship ties, and the moral expectations that shape behavior. These stories provide guidance on how to maintain relationships, resolve conflicts, and live in harmony with others and the natural world.

For example, in many First Nations communities in Canada, stories about the trickster figure (often referred to as Raven or Coyote) teach important lessons about human behavior, responsibility, and the consequences of violating social norms. Through these narratives, listeners learn about the values of honesty, respect, and accountability, which are central to restorative justice practices.

2. Preservation of Legal Traditions and Dispute Resolution Methods

Indigenous legal traditions are often embedded in oral narratives that convey the principles of justice, fairness, and conflict resolution. In these stories, the process of resolving disputes is not seen as a rigid set of rules but as a dynamic and evolving practice that is deeply connected to the community's values. Oral traditions provide a framework for understanding how to address wrongdoing, restore balance, and repair relationships.

Elders often use stories to convey traditional methods of dispute resolution, such as peacemaking, mediation, or restorative circles. These narratives illustrate how past generations have successfully navigated conflicts and how contemporary communities can continue to draw upon these practices to maintain social harmony. For instance, in the Navajo Nation, peacemaking is rooted in oral traditions that emphasize reconciliation, forgiveness, and the restoration of relationships, all of which are conveyed through stories passed down through the generations.

3. Spiritual and Cosmological Dimensions of Justice

Many Indigenous stories are deeply connected to spirituality and cosmology, reflecting the belief that justice is not only about human relationships but also about maintaining balance with the natural world and the spiritual realm. These stories often feature animals, ancestors, and spiritual beings who serve as moral exemplars or guides, teaching the community about the importance of living in harmony with the earth and with each other.

In the Māori tradition of New Zealand, for example, oral stories often emphasize the concept of whanaungatanga (kinship and connectedness), which extends beyond human relationships to include the natural environment and ancestors. Justice, in this context, is about maintaining balance and harmony across all aspects of life—something that is continuously reinforced through oral storytelling.

Storytelling as a Tool for Restorative Justice

In Indigenous communities, storytelling plays a central role in restorative justice practices. Stories are used to teach, guide, and heal, helping individuals and communities process harm, understand the impact of wrongdoing, and work toward reconciliation. By sharing stories, community members can engage in collective reflection, fostering empathy and understanding between victims, offenders, and the wider community.

1. Teaching Moral Lessons and Consequences

One of the most important functions of storytelling in Indigenous justice practices is to teach moral lessons. Stories about past events, mythological figures, or community leaders who exemplified virtues such as courage, wisdom, or humility are used to illustrate the importance of living according to communal values. These stories help individuals understand the consequences of their actions and the importance of taking responsibility for harm caused.

In many Indigenous restorative justice processes, offenders are invited to reflect on the lessons contained in traditional stories. For example, an elder might share a story about a character who caused harm but ultimately found redemption by making amends and restoring balance within the community. This encourages the offender to see their actions within a broader moral and cultural context and to consider how they can contribute to the healing process.

2. Facilitating Dialogue and Reflection

Storytelling is also used as a tool for facilitating dialogue in restorative justice settings. In many Indigenous cultures, justice processes are conducted in communal settings, such as circles or meetings, where all participants have an opportunity to speak and be heard. Storytelling helps create a space for reflection, allowing individuals to express their feelings and perspectives in a way that fosters mutual understanding.

In circle sentencing or peacemaking processes, elders and community members often begin by sharing stories that illustrate key themes of forgiveness, accountability, and healing. These stories set the tone for the discussion and encourage participants to approach the process with openness and a willingness to listen. By grounding the conversation in shared cultural narratives, storytelling helps create an atmosphere of respect and empathy, which is essential for successful restorative justice outcomes.

3. Healing and Reconciliation

Storytelling plays a vital role in the healing process for both victims and offenders. For victims, hearing stories about others who have experienced similar harm and found healing can provide comfort and hope. It reminds them that they are not alone and that the community is committed to supporting their recovery. For offenders, stories about accountability and redemption can inspire them to take meaningful steps toward making amends and reintegrating into the community.

In some Indigenous communities, stories about ancestors or spiritual figures are used to frame the justice process in a way that emphasizes healing over punishment. By connecting the justice process to spiritual and cultural traditions, storytelling helps participants understand that justice is not about retribution but about restoring balance and ensuring the well-being of all members of the community.

Oral Traditions and Contemporary Restorative Justice Practices

As Indigenous communities work to revitalize their legal traditions and assert their right to self-determination, oral storytelling continues to play a key role in contemporary restorative justice practices. In many cases, Indigenous restorative justice programs that have been integrated into formal legal systems still rely on storytelling as a core component of the process.

1. Circle Sentencing and Peacemaking Circles

In restorative justice processes like circle sentencing and peacemaking circles, storytelling remains a vital tool for fostering dialogue and understanding. Elders often share traditional stories at the beginning of a circle session, setting the stage for a thoughtful and respectful conversation. These stories help participants frame the discussion within the context of shared values, emphasizing the importance of community, healing, and accountability.

2. Truth and Reconciliation Commissions

In recent decades, Truth and Reconciliation Commissions (TRCs) in countries like Canada, South Africa, and Australia have highlighted the importance of oral testimony and storytelling as a means of addressing historical injustices. In these processes, Indigenous survivors of residential schools, land dispossession, and other colonial harms have shared their stories with the broader public, helping to educate others about the impact of colonialism and promote healing.

Storytelling in TRCs serves a dual purpose: it provides a platform for survivors to be heard and acknowledged, and it creates an opportunity for the wider society to learn from these stories and work toward reconciliation. By centering the voices of Indigenous peoples in the justice process, TRCs reflect the power of oral traditions as a tool for healing and collective reflection.

Conclusion: Storytelling as a Pillar of Restorative Justice

Oral traditions and storytelling are central to Indigenous restorative practices, serving as tools for teaching, healing, and reconciliation. Through stories, Indigenous communities transmit knowledge, preserve cultural values, and maintain social cohesion. In the context of restorative justice, storytelling helps individuals and communities process harm, reflect on moral lessons, and work toward the restoration of relationships.

As Indigenous peoples continue to revitalize their legal traditions and assert their rights, storytelling remains a vital part of the justice process. Whether in the form of traditional narratives, personal testimonies, or communal dialogue, storytelling provides a framework for understanding justice not as retribution, but as a means of healing, reconciliation, and the restoration of peace.

The Role of Storytelling in Indigenous Restorative Practices

2.2 The Power of Community Narratives in Justice

Community narratives are central to the fabric of Indigenous justice systems, embodying the collective memory, cultural identity, and shared values of the people. In many Indigenous communities, justice is viewed not as an individual or isolated process but as a collective endeavor in which the entire community is involved. Narratives passed down through generations serve as more than stories; they function as legal, moral, and social frameworks that guide decision-making, conflict resolution, and the maintenance of peace. These narratives shape the community's understanding of justice and inform restorative practices that aim to heal relationships, restore harmony, and reinforce communal ties.

By situating justice within the context of community narratives, Indigenous peoples ensure that legal processes are deeply connected to the shared values and lived experiences of their communities. These narratives provide a moral compass, offering insights into how conflicts have been handled in the past and setting a precedent for how future conflicts can be resolved. This chapter explores the critical role that community narratives play in shaping justice processes within Indigenous restorative frameworks, emphasizing their power to foster healing, accountability, and social cohesion.

The Role of Community Narratives in Shaping Collective Identity

Community narratives are more than a collection of stories; they are the collective memory of a people. These narratives contain the values, norms, and beliefs that define a community's identity, serving as a foundation for understanding justice and social order. In Indigenous societies, justice is not merely about the punishment of wrongdoers but about the restoration of harmony within the community. This focus on harmony is deeply rooted in the community's shared narratives, which reflect a worldview centered on interconnectedness, mutual responsibility, and the importance of relationships.

1. Collective Memory and Moral Guidance

Community narratives often serve as repositories of collective memory, recounting the events, decisions, and actions of ancestors who faced similar challenges. Through these narratives, community members are reminded of past wrongs, how they were addressed, and the outcomes of those justice processes. These stories provide moral guidance, offering lessons about accountability, forgiveness, and reconciliation. When conflicts arise, community members can draw upon these narratives to inform their decisions, ensuring that justice is administered in a way that aligns with the values and experiences of the community.

For example, many Indigenous communities tell stories about ancestral leaders who demonstrated wisdom and fairness in resolving conflicts. These stories are not merely historical accounts; they offer moral guidance for contemporary justice processes by illustrating the virtues of patience, empathy, and collective responsibility. Community members are encouraged to embody these qualities when addressing conflicts, ensuring that justice is administered with compassion and foresight.

2. Reinforcing Cultural Identity and Social Cohesion

Community narratives also play a crucial role in reinforcing cultural identity. By recounting the stories of ancestors, cultural heroes, and mythological figures, Indigenous peoples maintain a strong sense of who they are and where they come from. This shared identity is essential to the functioning of Indigenous justice systems, which rely on the participation and cooperation of the entire community. In many Indigenous cultures, the strength of the justice process is directly tied to the strength of the community itself. A cohesive, unified community is better able to address conflicts, restore harmony, and support both victims and offenders in the healing process.

These narratives often highlight the importance of relationships and interconnectedness, reminding community members that they are part of a larger whole. In many Indigenous traditions, harm done to one individual is seen as harm done to the entire community. Community narratives emphasize the importance of repairing these relationships and restoring the balance that has been disrupted by wrongdoing.

Community Narratives as Legal and Moral Frameworks

Indigenous justice systems are often based on principles derived from community narratives. These narratives provide a framework for understanding what is considered just or unjust, how conflicts should be resolved, and what is required to restore harmony after harm has been done. Rather than relying on written laws or codified legal procedures, Indigenous justice processes are grounded in the values and principles conveyed through oral traditions.

1. Narratives as Customary Law

In many Indigenous cultures, customary law is conveyed through community narratives. These stories contain important lessons about rights, responsibilities, and appropriate behavior within the community. They also outline the consequences of failing to uphold these responsibilities, offering guidance on how to address wrongdoing and restore balance.

For example, in some Indigenous communities, stories about the consequences of greed, dishonesty, or violence serve as cautionary tales, reminding community members of the importance of living in accordance with communal values. These stories function as a form of customary law, setting expectations for behavior and providing a framework for resolving disputes. When conflicts arise, community members can refer to these narratives to guide their decisions, ensuring that justice is administered in a way that aligns with cultural values.

2. Restorative Justice and Storytelling as Healing

Indigenous justice systems are deeply restorative, focusing on healing the harm caused by wrongdoing rather than merely punishing the offender. Community narratives play a key role in this restorative process, offering examples of how conflicts have been resolved in the past and providing a roadmap for reconciliation. These stories emphasize the importance of taking responsibility for one's actions, making amends, and restoring relationships.

In many restorative justice processes, community members, including victims, offenders, and elders, come together to share stories that help frame the conflict within the broader context of the community's shared values. These stories provide a space for reflection, allowing participants to understand the impact of their actions and work toward healing. By grounding the justice process in community narratives, Indigenous restorative practices ensure that justice is not only about resolving the immediate conflict but also about reinforcing the values and principles that sustain the community over time.

3. Intergenerational Knowledge Sharing and Justice

Community narratives are passed down from one generation to the next, ensuring that the knowledge and wisdom of ancestors continue to inform contemporary justice processes. This intergenerational transmission of knowledge is critical to the functioning of Indigenous justice systems, as it ensures that younger generations understand their responsibilities to the community and are equipped to participate in the justice process.

Elders play a central role in this knowledge-sharing process. As the keepers of community narratives, they are responsible for passing on the stories, customs, and values that define the community's approach to justice. When conflicts arise, elders often share stories that illustrate how similar situations were resolved in the past, offering guidance on how to move forward. This intergenerational transmission of knowledge helps ensure continuity in the justice process, reinforcing the values of accountability, healing, and reconciliation.

The Role of Community Narratives in Conflict Resolution

Community narratives not only shape the broader framework of justice in Indigenous communities but also play a practical role in resolving specific conflicts. When a conflict arises, community members often come together in a circle or other communal setting to share stories that relate to the issue at hand. These stories help frame the conflict within the context of the community's shared values and provide guidance on how to resolve it.

1. Storytelling as a Conflict Resolution Tool

In many Indigenous cultures, storytelling is an integral part of the conflict resolution process. When a dispute occurs, community members often gather to share stories that help participants reflect on the broader implications of the conflict. These stories may highlight the importance of forgiveness, accountability, or reconciliation, encouraging participants to approach the conflict with empathy and understanding.

For example, in circle sentencing or peacemaking processes, elders often begin by sharing stories that relate to the values of the community and the importance of restoring harmony. These stories help set the tone for the discussion, reminding participants of their shared responsibility to address the conflict in a way that promotes healing and reinforces communal ties.

2. Restoring Relationships Through Narrative

Indigenous justice systems prioritize the restoration of relationships, recognizing that harm caused by wrongdoing affects not only the individuals involved but also the broader community. Community narratives play a key role in this process by providing a framework for understanding how relationships can be repaired. Stories about reconciliation, forgiveness, and the reintegration of offenders offer practical guidance for restoring relationships and ensuring that both victims and offenders can move forward in peace.

For offenders, hearing stories about others who have taken responsibility for their actions and found redemption can inspire them to make amends and seek forgiveness. For victims, hearing stories about healing and reconciliation can provide comfort and help them understand that the community is committed to supporting their recovery. By connecting the justice process to these broader narratives, Indigenous restorative practices help ensure that justice is not only about resolving the immediate conflict but also about restoring harmony within the community.

Conclusion: The Power of Community Narratives in Justice

Community narratives are a powerful tool for shaping justice processes in Indigenous communities. These narratives serve as the foundation for customary law, moral guidance, and conflict resolution, offering a framework for understanding justice that is deeply connected to the shared values and experiences of the community. By grounding the justice process in these narratives, Indigenous restorative practices ensure that justice is not only about addressing wrongdoing but also about reinforcing the social and cultural fabric of the community.

Through storytelling, community members can reflect on past experiences, learn from the wisdom of ancestors, and work together to restore harmony. In doing so, Indigenous justice systems offer a powerful alternative to punitive models of justice, emphasizing healing, accountability, and the restoration of relationships. As Indigenous communities continue to revitalize their legal traditions, community narratives will remain central to the process of justice, ensuring that future generations are guided by the values of empathy, reconciliation, and collective responsibility.

The Role of Storytelling in Indigenous Restorative Practices

2.3 Healing Through Stories: Case Studies

Stories are not just tools for passing down knowledge in Indigenous communities—they are also central to the healing process in restorative justice practices. Through storytelling, Indigenous peoples address harm, promote healing, and restore social harmony within their communities. By sharing narratives that illustrate themes of accountability, forgiveness, and reconciliation, individuals are able to reflect on their actions, recognize the impact of harm, and work toward repairing relationships.

This section highlights case studies from various Indigenous communities where storytelling has played a transformative role in the restorative justice process. These examples illustrate how storytelling fosters healing, supports reconciliation, and strengthens community bonds by helping individuals understand the broader implications of their actions and by guiding them toward making meaningful reparations.

Case Study 1: Navajo Peacemaking (Southwestern United States)

The Navajo Nation's Peacemaking Program is one of the most well-known examples of how storytelling is integrated into Indigenous restorative justice. This traditional system focuses on repairing relationships and restoring harmony, not only for the individuals involved in the conflict but for the entire community. At the heart of the peacemaking process is storytelling, where participants are encouraged to share their stories and listen to the stories of others, creating a space for empathy, reflection, and healing.

Storytelling in the Peacemaking Process

In Navajo peacemaking, all participants, including the victim, the offender, family members, and community elders, sit together in a circle. The peacemaker, often an elder who is deeply respected for their wisdom, begins by sharing a traditional story that relates to the nature of the conflict. These stories are usually drawn from Navajo oral traditions and highlight key values such as balance, respect, and responsibility. The story sets the tone for the discussion, reminding participants of the importance of healing and reconciliation.

For example, a common story shared in peacemaking circles might involve Hózhó, the Navajo concept of harmony and balance in the universe. The story could emphasize how actions that disrupt harmony—whether through anger, violence, or dishonesty—create disharmony in the community. The offender is encouraged to reflect on how their actions disrupted the Hózhó of the community and to take steps toward restoring that balance.

Impact of Storytelling on Healing

In this process, storytelling allows both the victim and the offender to share their personal narratives. The victim's story is heard with empathy and validation, while the offender's story often provides context for their actions, fostering understanding and reducing animosity. Hearing the stories of others enables participants to recognize the broader social and emotional dimensions of the conflict.

In one case, a young man who had been involved in a violent altercation participated in a peacemaking session. Through storytelling, the victim was able to express how the violence had impacted their sense of safety and well-being, while the offender shared a story of personal struggles, including loss and hardship, that had contributed to the incident. The process of listening to each other's stories created a space for mutual understanding, allowing both parties to empathize with each other and work toward reconciliation.

By the end of the peacemaking process, the offender agreed to make amends through community service and expressed a desire to help younger community members avoid similar situations. The victim, having been heard and validated, agreed to the terms of reconciliation, and the community as a whole was able to move forward in peace.

Case Study 2: Circle Sentencing in First Nations Communities (Canada)

Circle sentencing is a restorative justice practice used in many First Nations communities in Canada. It draws on traditional Indigenous methods of conflict resolution and emphasizes the role of the community in addressing harm. A key component of circle sentencing is storytelling, where participants share their experiences and feelings, contributing to a process of collective healing.

Storytelling and Community Involvement

In a circle sentencing process, the circle includes the victim, the offender, their families, community members, and sometimes law enforcement officials or judges. The goal is to engage everyone in an open dialogue about the harm that has occurred and how it can be repaired. Storytelling is used throughout the process to foster understanding and support healing for all involved.

For example, in a case involving a young man who had committed theft in a small community, circle sentencing was employed to address the harm done. During the circle, the victim shared their story of how the theft had impacted their business and trust in the community, while the offender explained the personal and financial struggles that had led them to commit the crime. Community elders shared stories from the past about similar situations, where individuals had taken responsibility for their actions and worked to restore trust.

These shared stories helped the offender realize the broader consequences of their actions and the importance of making amends. The victim, in turn, gained a better understanding of the offender's situation, which helped to soften their anger and create space for forgiveness. The community as a whole was involved in creating a plan for restitution, which included the offender working to repair the damage caused by the theft.

Healing Through Shared Stories

In circle sentencing, storytelling plays a crucial role in helping both victims and offenders process their emotions. For victims, sharing their story allows them to express the full impact of the harm, while also receiving support from the community. For offenders, storytelling helps them understand the consequences of their actions and offers them a chance to take responsibility in a way that promotes healing and reconciliation, rather than simply punishment.

In this case, after hearing the victim's story, the offender apologized and agreed to perform community service to repay the harm caused. The process also helped the offender feel supported in their efforts to change, as community members offered encouragement and guidance for their future actions. This approach to justice not only repaired the harm but also strengthened the social fabric of the community, reinforcing the values of accountability and mutual support.

Case Study 3: Māori Whānau Conferencing (New Zealand)

In Māori communities in New Zealand, the practice of whānau conferencing (family group conferencing) is a restorative justice process that brings together the extended family, or whānau, of both the victim and the offender to address harm and seek resolution. This process, rooted in Māori customs and traditions, heavily relies on storytelling to facilitate dialogue and healing.

Storytelling in Whānau Conferencing

Whānau conferencing is based on the belief that conflicts affect not only the individuals involved but also their families and the broader community. During the conference, participants are encouraged to share their stories about the conflict, its impact, and their hopes for resolution. Elders often play a central role in guiding the process, sharing stories that illustrate the importance of values such as mana (respect, dignity) and whakapapa (ancestral connections).

In one case, a whānau conference was held to address a situation involving a young person who had vandalized community property. During the conference, the young person's parents shared stories about the struggles their child had faced, including peer pressure and feelings of alienation. The elders then shared stories from Māori traditions about individuals who had overcome challenges and restored their mana through acts of service and responsibility.

The victim's family also shared stories about how the vandalism had affected their pride in the community and their sense of connection to the land. Through this exchange of stories, both the offender and the victim's families were able to see the situation from each other's perspectives, fostering empathy and understanding.

Restoring Harmony Through Storytelling

By the end of the whānau conference, a plan for restitution was agreed upon that included the young person repairing the damage they had caused and participating in community activities to rebuild trust. The process of sharing stories helped the young person take responsibility for their actions, while also allowing both families to move forward in a spirit of forgiveness and reconciliation.

In this case, storytelling was a powerful tool for healing because it allowed participants to connect their personal experiences with broader cultural narratives about responsibility, dignity, and community. The process reinforced the importance of collective responsibility and the need to restore harmony within the community.

Conclusion: The Healing Power of Stories

These case studies demonstrate the profound role that storytelling plays in Indigenous restorative justice practices. By sharing stories, both victims and offenders are able to process their emotions, understand the broader context of their actions, and work toward healing and reconciliation. Stories provide a framework for reflecting on the impact of harm, taking responsibility, and making amends, while also reinforcing the cultural values that sustain the community.

In each of these examples, storytelling is not just a tool for resolving conflicts—it is a means of restoring relationships, rebuilding trust, and ensuring the long-term health and well-being of the community. Through storytelling, Indigenous restorative justice practices offer a powerful alternative to punitive models of justice, emphasizing healing, accountability, and the restoration of balance.

CHAPTER 03

KEY CONCEPTS OF RESTORATIVE JUSTICE IN INDIGENOUS CONTEXT

3.1 Reparation, Healing, and Reconciliation

In Indigenous justice systems, the concepts of reparation, healing, and reconciliation are deeply intertwined. Justice is not solely about punishing wrongdoers but about repairing the harm caused, restoring balance within the community, and ensuring the long-term well-being of all affected parties. These core principles reflect the values of interconnectedness, collective responsibility, and respect that underpin Indigenous worldviews. By focusing on reparation, healing, and reconciliation, Indigenous restorative justice practices offer a powerful alternative to the punitive, retributive approaches common in many Western legal systems.

This chapter explores these three key concepts within Indigenous justice frameworks and highlights their significance in fostering long-term peace and social harmony.

Reparation: Addressing Harm and Making Amends

Reparation is central to Indigenous restorative justice processes. It involves addressing the harm caused by wrongdoing and taking steps to make amends, whether through material restitution, symbolic acts of reconciliation, or community service. In many Indigenous communities, reparation is not seen as a one-time act but as part of an ongoing process of restoring balance and repairing relationships. The goal is to ensure that the victim, the offender, and the community as a whole can heal from the harm caused and move forward together.

Forms of Reparation in Indigenous Contexts

1. Material Reparation

Material reparation may involve compensating the victim for any financial loss or damage caused by the offense. This can include replacing stolen goods, paying for damages, or providing other forms of compensation that address the material impact of the harm. However, in Indigenous justice systems, material reparation is often supplemented by other forms of amends that are more symbolic or communal in nature.

2. Symbolic Reparation

In addition to material restitution, symbolic reparation plays a significant role in Indigenous justice practices. Symbolic acts, such as offering a formal apology, participating in ceremonies, or engaging in acts of community service, are often required to restore the moral and social balance that has been disrupted by wrongdoing. These acts help demonstrate the offender's commitment to making amends and reintegrating into the community.

For example, in many First Nations communities, offenders may be asked to participate in a ceremonial healing circle or undertake specific tasks that contribute to the well-being of the community. These symbolic gestures are designed to repair not only the immediate harm but also the broader social and spiritual damage caused by the offense.

3. Community-Based Reparation

In Indigenous justice systems, harm is often viewed as something that affects the entire community, not just the individual victim. As a result, reparation frequently involves acts that benefit the wider community. Offenders may be required to engage in community service, such as helping to organize community events, maintaining communal spaces, or assisting elders. By contributing to the well-being of the community, offenders demonstrate their commitment to making amends and rebuilding trust.

Community-based reparation also serves as a way to reintegrate offenders into the social fabric of the community. Rather than isolating the offender through punishment, Indigenous justice practices emphasize reintegration, ensuring that the individual can continue to contribute to the health and harmony of the community.

The Role of Elders in Facilitating Reparation

Elders play a central role in facilitating the reparation process in many Indigenous communities. As keepers of cultural knowledge and moral authority, elders guide offenders through the process of making amends, offering wisdom and support as they work to repair the harm caused. Elders may also work with victims and their families to ensure that the reparation process meets their needs and leads to healing.

Elders often determine the appropriate forms of reparation based on cultural traditions and the specific circumstances of the offense. Their involvement ensures that the process is rooted in the community's values and that both victims and offenders feel supported throughout the process.

Healing: Addressing the Emotional and Spiritual Impact of Harm

Healing is a key goal of Indigenous restorative justice practices. Justice is not seen as complete until the emotional, psychological, and spiritual wounds caused by wrongdoing have been addressed. Healing is not only for the victim but for the offender and the broader community as well. The aim is to ensure that all parties affected by the harm are able to move forward with a sense of closure, peace, and restored relationships.

Healing for Victims

For victims, healing is an essential part of the justice process. Indigenous restorative justice practices provide space for victims to share their stories, express their emotions, and have their experiences validated by the community. This process of being heard and acknowledged is a crucial step toward healing, as it helps victims regain a sense of control and agency after experiencing harm.

In some Indigenous communities, healing ceremonies or rituals are conducted to help victims process their emotions and move forward. These ceremonies may involve prayers, songs, or the participation of spiritual leaders who help guide the victim through the healing process. By framing justice within a spiritual and communal context, Indigenous practices ensure that healing is holistic and addresses the victim's emotional, psychological, and spiritual needs.

Healing for Offenders

In Indigenous justice systems, healing is also extended to the offender. The goal is not simply to punish but to help the offender recognize the harm they have caused, take responsibility, and make meaningful changes in their behavior. By engaging in the reparation process and participating in restorative justice practices, offenders have the opportunity to heal from any personal issues that may have contributed to their wrongdoing.

Healing for offenders often involves reflecting on their actions, understanding the broader impact of their behavior, and engaging in dialogue with victims and community members. This process helps offenders reconnect with the values of the community and restore their relationships with others. In many cases, the healing process is facilitated by elders, who provide guidance and support as the offender works toward making amends.

Community Healing

Indigenous restorative justice practices recognize that harm affects not only the victim and the offender but also the entire community. When wrongdoing occurs, it creates a ripple effect, disrupting the balance and harmony of the community. As a result, justice processes often involve the participation of the broader community in healing.

Community healing may take the form of public ceremonies, communal dialogues, or collective acts of reparation. These practices help rebuild trust, reinforce social bonds, and ensure that the community as a whole can move forward in peace. By involving the entire community in the healing process, Indigenous justice systems strengthen the social fabric and promote long-term harmony.

Reconciliation: Restoring Relationships and Social Harmony

Reconciliation is the ultimate goal of Indigenous restorative justice practices. It involves restoring relationships that have been damaged by wrongdoing and ensuring that all parties can move forward in peace and harmony. Reconciliation is not just about resolving the immediate conflict but about rebuilding trust and ensuring that the offender is reintegrated into the community as a valued member.

The Role of Dialogue in Reconciliation

Reconciliation is often facilitated through open dialogue between the victim, the offender, and the community. These dialogues may take place in circles, where participants have the opportunity to share their perspectives, express their emotions, and work together to find a resolution. The process is guided by principles of respect, empathy, and collective responsibility, ensuring that all voices are heard and that the needs of all parties are addressed.

In many Indigenous cultures, reconciliation is not seen as a one-time event but as an ongoing process. Even after formal justice processes have been completed, the community continues to support both the victim and the offender as they work to rebuild their relationships. This long-term commitment to reconciliation ensures that the social and emotional wounds caused by wrongdoing are fully healed.

Reintegration of Offenders

Reconciliation in Indigenous justice systems is closely linked to the reintegration of offenders. Once an offender has taken responsibility for their actions and made amends, the community works to reintegrate them as a valued member. This reintegration is essential for restoring social harmony and preventing further harm. Rather than isolating or stigmatizing the offender, Indigenous justice practices focus on helping them repair relationships and contribute to the well-being of the community.

For offenders, reintegration often involves participating in community activities, fulfilling responsibilities, and demonstrating a commitment to positive change. By welcoming offenders back into the community, Indigenous justice practices help prevent recidivism and promote long-term peace.

Conclusion: The Interconnectedness of Reparation, Healing, and Reconciliation

Reparation, healing, and reconciliation are core concepts in Indigenous restorative justice systems. These processes are deeply interconnected, reflecting the values of community, responsibility, and interconnectedness that underpin Indigenous worldviews. By focusing on repairing harm, addressing emotional and spiritual wounds, and restoring relationships, Indigenous justice practices offer a holistic and compassionate approach to justice.

These key concepts emphasize that justice is not about punishment but about restoring balance and ensuring the well-being of all members of the community. Through reparation, healing, and reconciliation, Indigenous restorative justice practices create the conditions for lasting peace, social cohesion, and collective well-being. As we continue to explore these practices, it becomes clear that they offer valuable lessons for creating more just and compassionate societies.

Key Concepts of Restorative Justice in Indigenous Contexts

3.2 The Role of Elders and Community Leadership

Elders and community leaders play an essential role in Indigenous restorative justice practices. They serve as the guardians of cultural knowledge, the facilitators of conflict resolution, and the moral compass for the community. Their authority and wisdom, rooted in tradition and lived experience, guide the justice process in a way that is both culturally relevant and deeply connected to the values of the community.

In Indigenous justice systems, the role of elders and community leaders extends far beyond that of judges or arbitrators in Western legal contexts. Instead of simply determining guilt or innocence, these leaders act as facilitators of healing, reconciliation, and social harmony. They help to mediate disputes, support victims, and guide offenders in taking responsibility for their actions. Through their involvement, elders ensure that justice is not only about addressing individual wrongs but also about maintaining the collective well-being of the community.

This chapter explores the multifaceted role of elders and community leadership in Indigenous restorative justice practices, examining how their guidance ensures that justice processes are deeply rooted in cultural traditions and promote long-term healing and harmony.

The Central Role of Elders in Indigenous Justice

Elders are revered figures in many Indigenous communities, seen as the keepers of cultural knowledge and spiritual wisdom. Their role in justice processes is crucial because they embody the values, customs, and traditions that have sustained Indigenous societies for generations. In restorative justice practices, elders often serve as mediators, facilitators, and advisors, ensuring that conflicts are resolved in a way that aligns with the community's values and promotes healing for all parties involved.

1. Custodians of Cultural Knowledge

Elders are the custodians of Indigenous legal traditions, which are often passed down orally from generation to generation. Their knowledge of customary law, conflict resolution practices, and cultural values makes them uniquely qualified to guide the justice process. In many Indigenous communities, formal legal codes are less important than the wisdom of elders, who interpret and apply traditional knowledge to address contemporary conflicts.

Elders draw upon stories, teachings, and past experiences to offer guidance in justice processes. They help community members understand the broader social and spiritual implications of wrongdoing, emphasizing the importance of restoring balance and harmony. Their deep connection to the community's history and values allows them to offer solutions that are culturally appropriate and effective.

2. Mediators and Facilitators of Dialogue

In Indigenous justice systems, elders often take on the role of mediators, facilitating dialogue between victims, offenders, and the broader community. Their presence lends authority and legitimacy to the justice process, ensuring that all parties approach the discussion with respect and a willingness to listen. Elders create a safe and supportive space for open dialogue, allowing participants to share their stories, express their emotions, and work toward reconciliation.

For example, in many Indigenous communities, elders lead peacemaking circles or healing circles, where victims, offenders, and community members come together to address harm. The elder begins the process by sharing a story or teaching that relates to the conflict, setting the tone for the discussion and reminding participants of the community's values. By guiding the conversation with empathy and wisdom, elders help participants move beyond blame and toward understanding, accountability, and healing.

3. Moral and Spiritual Leadership

Elders also serve as moral and spiritual leaders within the justice process. Their deep connection to Indigenous spirituality allows them to guide participants through the emotional and spiritual aspects of conflict resolution. In many

Indigenous cultures, wrongdoing is not only seen as a violation of social norms but also as a disruption of the spiritual harmony between individuals, the community, and the natural world. Elders help restore this balance by incorporating spiritual practices, such as prayers, ceremonies, or rituals, into the justice process.

For instance, in the Navajo Peacemaking tradition, elders often invoke the concept of Hózhó—a Navajo term meaning harmony, balance, and beauty. They remind participants that wrongdoing disrupts Hózhó and that the goal of the justice process is to restore this harmony. Through their spiritual guidance, elders help participants recognize the broader impact of their actions and encourage them to take responsibility for restoring balance within the community.

The Role of Community Leaders in Indigenous Restorative Justice

In addition to elders, community leaders—such as chiefs, clan leaders, and other respected figures—play a crucial role in Indigenous restorative justice processes. These leaders are often responsible for upholding the social order, maintaining relationships between families and clans, and ensuring the well-being of the community. Like elders, community leaders act as facilitators of justice, helping to mediate disputes, ensure fairness, and promote healing.

1. Maintaining Social Order and Harmony

Community leaders in Indigenous societies have long been responsible for maintaining social order and resolving conflicts. Their leadership is rooted in a deep understanding of the interconnectedness of individuals, families, and the broader community. When conflicts arise, these leaders are often called upon to intervene, not as enforcers of punishment but as facilitators of reconciliation and healing.

For example, in Māori communities in New Zealand, community leaders play a central role in whānau (family group) conferencing, a restorative justice process that brings together the victim, the offender, and their families to discuss the harm caused and seek a resolution. The community leader acts as a facilitator, ensuring that the process is fair, respectful, and focused on restoring relationships. By promoting dialogue and mutual understanding, these leaders help the community move forward in a spirit of reconciliation.

2. Upholding Collective Responsibility

In Indigenous justice systems, responsibility for addressing harm is often shared by the entire community, rather than being placed solely on the individual offender. Community leaders help uphold this principle of collective responsibility by involving the broader community in the justice process. They ensure that victims, offenders, and their families all participate in the resolution of the conflict and contribute to the healing process.

This collective approach to justice reflects the belief that wrongdoing affects not only the individuals involved but also the entire community. By involving the community in the justice process, leaders reinforce the idea that everyone has a role to play in restoring harmony and ensuring that similar conflicts do not arise in the future. This shared responsibility helps strengthen social bonds and promotes long-term peace.

3. Supporting Reconciliation and Reintegration

Community leaders are also responsible for supporting the reintegration of offenders into the community after they have taken responsibility for their actions and made amends. In Indigenous justice systems, the goal is not to punish or isolate offenders but to help them heal, learn from their mistakes, and reintegrate as productive members of the community. Community leaders play a key role in this reintegration process by providing guidance, support, and opportunities for offenders to contribute to the well-being of the community.

For instance, in some First Nations communities in Canada, community leaders may organize circle sentencing processes, where offenders participate in a circle with victims, community members, and elders. The goal of the circle is to determine how the offender can make amends and reintegrate into the community. Community leaders help facilitate this process, ensuring that the resolution is fair and that the offender is supported in their efforts to change.

Challenges Faced by Elders and Community Leaders in Modern Justice Systems

While elders and community leaders play a central role in Indigenous justice processes, they face significant challenges in modern contexts, particularly when Indigenous justice practices intersect with formal legal systems. These challenges include the marginalization of Indigenous legal traditions, the imposition of Western legal frameworks, and the difficulties of maintaining cultural continuity in the face of external pressures.

1. Marginalization of Indigenous Legal Traditions

In many countries, Indigenous legal traditions have been marginalized or suppressed by colonial and post-colonial governments. Western legal systems, which prioritize punitive justice and individual rights, often fail to recognize the value of Indigenous restorative justice practices, which focus on healing, reconciliation, and community involvement. As a result, elders and community leaders may struggle to assert the legitimacy of their justice practices within formal legal frameworks.

2. Integration with Western Legal Systems

In recent years, there has been a growing movement to integrate Indigenous restorative justice practices into formal legal systems. While this has led to some positive outcomes, it also presents challenges for elders and community leaders, who must navigate the complexities of working within a legal system that may not fully align with Indigenous values. Elders and leaders may find themselves having to adapt their practices to meet the requirements of the formal legal system, which can dilute the cultural integrity of the process.

3. Cultural Continuity and Modernization

The pressures of modernization, urbanization, and globalization also pose challenges for maintaining cultural continuity in Indigenous justice practices. Younger generations may be less connected to traditional customs and values, and the role of elders and community leaders may be diminished in urban settings where Indigenous communities are more dispersed. Despite these challenges, many Indigenous communities are actively working to revitalize their legal traditions and ensure that elders and community leaders remain central to the justice process.

Conclusion: The Essential Role of Elders and Community Leadership

Elders and community leaders are the backbone of Indigenous restorative justice systems. Their wisdom, cultural knowledge, and spiritual guidance ensure that justice processes are deeply rooted in tradition and focused on healing, reconciliation, and the restoration of balance. By facilitating dialogue, supporting victims and offenders, and maintaining social harmony, elders and leaders help to sustain the values of the community and promote long-term peace.

As Indigenous justice systems continue to evolve and adapt to modern challenges, the role of elders and community leadership remains crucial. Their involvement ensures that justice is not merely about addressing individual wrongs but about fostering collective healing, strengthening social bonds, and upholding the cultural and spiritual integrity of the community. Through their leadership, Indigenous restorative justice practices offer a powerful model for creating more compassionate and equitable systems of justice.

Key Concepts of Restorative Justice in Indigenous Contexts

3.3 Integrating Spirituality and Restorative Practices

In Indigenous justice systems, spirituality is inseparable from the concepts of healing, reconciliation, and justice. Spiritual beliefs and practices provide a framework for understanding the world, one's place in it, and the responsibilities individuals have toward one another and the broader community. For many Indigenous communities, justice is not simply about resolving disputes or punishing wrongdoers; it is about restoring balance within the spiritual, social, and natural order.

Spirituality in Indigenous contexts often emphasizes interconnectedness—between people, the land, ancestors, and spiritual entities. When harm occurs, it is seen as a disruption to this interconnectedness, requiring more than material or physical reparation; it calls for a restoration of the spiritual and emotional balance of the community. Integrating spirituality into restorative justice processes allows for a more holistic approach, addressing not only the tangible effects of harm but also the spiritual wounds that result from wrongdoing.

This chapter explores how Indigenous justice systems integrate spirituality into restorative practices, focusing on how spiritual beliefs and ceremonies contribute to healing, reconciliation, and the restoration of community harmony.

Spiritual Foundations of Indigenous Justice

In many Indigenous cultures, justice is rooted in spiritual principles that emphasize balance, respect, and the interconnectedness of all life. These principles shape not only how conflicts are resolved but also how people understand their roles and responsibilities within the community. Spirituality is not a separate aspect of life; it permeates all aspects of existence, including how justice is administered.

1. Spirituality as a Guide for Justice

Indigenous spirituality often views the world as a web of interconnected relationships between humans, the natural world, and spiritual entities. Harm or wrongdoing is seen as a disruption of these relationships, creating imbalance not only in the material realm but also in the spiritual and social realms. Restorative justice practices seek to repair this imbalance by addressing the spiritual dimensions of harm, allowing individuals and communities to heal on a deeper level.

For example, in many Native American and First Nations traditions, justice is closely tied to concepts of harmony and balance. When a conflict or crime occurs, it is understood as a disturbance to the natural and spiritual order, requiring a process of reconciliation that restores not only relationships between people but also the community's relationship with the spiritual world. Elders and spiritual leaders often play a central role in guiding this process, using their knowledge of spiritual teachings to facilitate healing and reconciliation.

2. The Role of Ceremonies and Rituals

Ceremonies and rituals are central to the integration of spirituality into Indigenous restorative justice practices. These rituals help participants connect with spiritual teachings, ancestors, and the natural world, providing a sense of grounding and meaning in the justice process. Ceremonies often serve as moments of reflection, forgiveness, and reconciliation, allowing individuals to move forward with a sense of spiritual closure.

Ceremonies may take various forms, depending on the specific cultural and spiritual traditions of the community. In some cases, they involve prayers, songs, dances, or offerings to spiritual entities. These practices are not only symbolic but also serve as tangible ways to address spiritual harm and facilitate healing. For example, in some Indigenous communities, purification ceremonies such as smudging are conducted to cleanse the emotional and spiritual energy of participants before a justice process begins. This allows both victims and offenders to enter the process with an open heart, ready to engage in meaningful dialogue and reconciliation.

3. The Role of Ancestors and Spiritual Entities

In Indigenous worldviews, ancestors and spiritual entities are often seen as active participants in the justice process. The wisdom of ancestors is invoked to guide decision-making, while spiritual entities are called upon to provide protection, insight, and support for those involved in the conflict. The involvement of ancestors and spiritual entities serves as a reminder that justice is not merely a human endeavor but a sacred process that affects the entire community, both living and deceased.

In Māori culture, for example, the concept of whakapapa (genealogy) emphasizes the connection between the individual and their ancestors. When harm occurs, it is seen as a disruption to the broader ancestral lineage, and the process of reconciliation often involves invoking the wisdom and guidance of ancestors. Similarly, in many Indigenous African traditions, spiritual rituals are performed to honor the ancestors and seek their intervention in resolving disputes.

By integrating the spiritual realm into justice practices, Indigenous communities ensure that justice is not only about addressing the immediate harm but also about maintaining harmony with the spiritual world.

Spiritual Healing in Restorative Justice Practices

The integration of spirituality into Indigenous justice systems allows for a more holistic approach to healing. Spiritual healing is concerned with repairing not only the physical or material damage caused by wrongdoing but also the emotional and spiritual wounds experienced by both victims and offenders. In many Indigenous cultures, the process of spiritual healing is seen as essential to restoring balance within the community.

1. Healing Circles and Spiritual Dialogue

Healing circles are a common restorative justice practice in many Indigenous communities. These circles bring together victims, offenders, elders, and community members in a spiritual setting to discuss the harm that has occurred and to work toward reconciliation. Healing circles are often conducted in sacred spaces and incorporate spiritual elements such as prayers, songs, and rituals.

One of the key aspects of healing circles is the use of spiritual dialogue, where participants are encouraged to reflect on the spiritual impact of the harm and to seek guidance from spiritual teachings. Elders or spiritual leaders facilitate these discussions, helping participants explore how their actions have disrupted the spiritual harmony of the community and how they can work to restore it.

For victims, healing circles provide a space to express their pain and seek spiritual healing for the trauma they have experienced. For offenders, the process helps them understand the broader spiritual consequences of their actions and take responsibility for making amends. By grounding the justice process in spirituality, healing circles foster a deeper sense of empathy, accountability, and reconciliation.

2. Ceremonial Apologies and Forgiveness

In many Indigenous cultures, forgiveness is a key component of the justice process. However, forgiveness is not seen as automatic or superficial; it is a deeply spiritual act that requires both the victim and the offender to engage in meaningful reflection and dialogue. Ceremonial apologies are often used to facilitate this process, allowing offenders to formally acknowledge their wrongdoing and seek forgiveness from the victim and the community.

These ceremonial apologies are often accompanied by rituals that emphasize the spiritual significance of the act of forgiveness. For example, in some First Nations communities in Canada, offenders may be required to participate in a public ceremony where they express their remorse and make amends. This may involve offering gifts, performing acts of service, or participating in a healing ritual that symbolizes the restoration of balance.

For victims, the process of forgiving is also seen as a spiritual act of letting go of anger and pain. Ceremonies may be performed to help victims release negative emotions and find peace, allowing them to move forward in their healing journey. By integrating spirituality into the act of forgiveness, Indigenous justice practices ensure that the process is meaningful and transformative for all involved.

3. Spiritual Reintegration of Offenders

In Indigenous justice systems, reintegration is not just about restoring the offender's place within the community; it is also about restoring their spiritual well-being. Offenders are often seen as spiritually wounded by their actions, and the justice process is designed to help them heal on a spiritual level so that they can re-enter the community in a positive and meaningful way.

Spiritual reintegration may involve participation in ceremonies that cleanse and purify the offender, allowing them to symbolically and spiritually leave behind their wrongdoing. In some cultures, offenders may participate in sweat lodge ceremonies, vision quests, or other spiritual rituals that help them reflect on their actions, seek forgiveness from the spiritual world, and prepare for a new chapter in their lives.

By focusing on spiritual reintegration, Indigenous justice practices ensure that offenders are not merely punished or shamed but are given the opportunity to heal, grow, and make positive contributions to the community.

Challenges and Opportunities for Integrating Spirituality into Modern Justice Systems

While the integration of spirituality is central to Indigenous justice systems, it can pose challenges when Indigenous practices intersect with formal, state-run legal systems. Western legal frameworks, which tend to prioritize secularism and punitive measures, may struggle to accommodate the spiritual dimensions of Indigenous justice. However, there are also opportunities for legal systems to learn from Indigenous practices and incorporate more holistic, restorative approaches to justice.

1. Recognizing the Value of Spirituality in Justice

One of the key challenges is the tendency of formal legal systems to view justice as a purely secular process. In many Western legal systems, justice is understood in terms of punishment, deterrence, and retribution, with little consideration given to the spiritual or emotional impact of harm. This can make it difficult for Indigenous communities to fully integrate their spiritual practices into state-run justice systems.

However, there is growing recognition of the value of spirituality in promoting healing and reconciliation. Some restorative justice programs have begun to incorporate elements of Indigenous spirituality, such as healing circles and ceremonial apologies, into their practices. These programs offer an opportunity to bridge the gap between secular and spiritual approaches to justice, creating a more holistic system that addresses the full range of human experiences.

2. Balancing Cultural Integrity with Legal Requirements

Another challenge is the need to balance the cultural integrity of Indigenous justice practices with the requirements of formal legal systems. While Indigenous communities may wish to maintain their spiritual traditions in justice processes, they may face pressure to conform to legal standards that prioritize evidence, procedure, and punishment over healing and reconciliation.

Despite these challenges, there are many examples of successful integration. In Canada, for instance, some courts allow Indigenous offenders to participate in traditional healing circles as part of their sentencing. These programs, which are overseen by elders and spiritual leaders, emphasize the spiritual dimensions of healing and reintegration, allowing offenders to take responsibility for their actions in a culturally meaningful way.

Conclusion: The Power of Spirituality in Indigenous Restorative Justice

Spirituality is a powerful force in Indigenous restorative justice practices, providing a framework for healing, reconciliation, and the restoration of balance within the community. By integrating spiritual beliefs, ceremonies, and rituals into the justice process, Indigenous communities ensure that justice addresses not only the material and emotional dimensions of harm but also the spiritual wounds that result from wrongdoing.

Through spiritual dialogue, healing ceremonies, and the guidance of elders and spiritual leaders, Indigenous justice practices offer a holistic approach to justice that fosters long-term healing and social harmony. As formal legal systems increasingly recognize the value of restorative justice, there is an opportunity to learn from Indigenous traditions and integrate more spiritual, compassionate approaches to addressing harm and promoting reconciliation.

CHAPTER 04

CASE STUDIES FROM INDIGENOUS COMMUNITIES

4.1 The Navajo Peacemaking System

The Navajo Peacemaking system is one of the most well-known examples of Indigenous restorative justice in practice. Rooted in the cultural and spiritual traditions of the Navajo people (Diné), Peacemaking serves as a restorative process that prioritizes healing, harmony, and community involvement over punishment. Rather than focusing on retribution, Navajo Peacemaking aims to resolve conflicts by addressing the root causes of harm, repairing relationships, and restoring the balance between individuals, families, and the broader community.

The Navajo term for Peacemaking is Hózhóji Naat'áanii, which refers to the process of restoring Hózhó—

a central concept in Navajo philosophy that represents beauty, harmony, balance, and well-being. When harm or conflict occurs, it disrupts the Hózhó of the community, and the goal of Peacemaking is to restore this harmony through dialogue, mutual understanding, and spiritual reflection.

This case study explores the history, principles, and process of the Navajo Peacemaking system, highlighting how it exemplifies Indigenous restorative justice practices. It also examines the challenges and successes of integrating Peacemaking with formal legal systems, particularly in the context of the Navajo Nation's unique status as a sovereign Indigenous nation within the United States.

Historical Context and Origins of Navajo Peacemaking

The Navajo Peacemaking system has its roots in ancient Navajo traditions of conflict resolution, which predate the arrival of European settlers in North America. Historically, the Navajo people used Peacemaking to resolve a wide range of disputes, including familial conflicts, community disagreements, and violations of cultural norms. The process was deeply embedded in Navajo spiritual beliefs, emphasizing the interconnectedness of individuals, the land, and the spiritual world.

Before the imposition of Western legal systems, the Navajo people maintained their own systems of governance and justice, with Peacemaking serving as a primary method for resolving conflicts. During colonization, however, Western-style courts and legal institutions were introduced, and Indigenous justice practices were marginalized. Despite this, the Navajo people continued to practice Peacemaking, preserving it as a vital aspect of their cultural identity and legal traditions.

In the late 20th century, the Navajo Nation began to formally integrate Peacemaking into its judicial system, recognizing it as a valuable alternative to adversarial court processes. Today, the Navajo Peacemaking system operates alongside the Navajo Nation court system, offering a culturally grounded method for resolving disputes within the Navajo community.

Key Principles of Navajo Peacemaking

The Navajo Peacemaking system is based on several key principles that distinguish it from Western adversarial justice systems. These principles reflect the values of harmony, interconnectedness, and collective responsibility that are central to Navajo culture.

1. Restoring Harmony and Balance (Hózhó)

At the heart of Navajo Peacemaking is the concept of Hózhó, which refers to the state of harmony, balance, and beauty that should exist in all aspects of life. When conflict or wrongdoing occurs, it is seen as a disruption of this harmony. The goal of Peacemaking is to restore Hózhó by addressing the root causes of the conflict, healing relationships, and ensuring that all parties can move forward in peace.

Unlike Western justice systems, which often focus on punishing the offender, Navajo Peacemaking emphasizes the importance of repairing relationships and restoring balance within the community. This restorative approach ensures that justice is not only about resolving the immediate conflict but also about promoting long-term harmony.

2. Involvement of the Entire Community

Navajo Peacemaking is a communal process that involves not only the victim and the offender but also their families, community members, and spiritual leaders. The entire community has a stake in the resolution of the conflict, as the disruption caused by wrongdoing affects everyone. By involving the community in the justice process, Peacemaking fosters collective responsibility and ensures that the resolution reflects the values and needs of the community as a whole.

The Peacemaking process is guided by a Peacemaker, who is usually an elder or respected community leader. The Peacemaker facilitates dialogue between the parties, helping them identify the underlying issues that led to the conflict and working toward a solution that restores harmony. This inclusive approach ensures that all voices are heard and that the resolution is supported by the broader community.

3. Spiritual Reflection and Reconciliation

Spirituality is central to the Navajo Peacemaking process. Participants are encouraged to reflect on the spiritual dimensions of the conflict, considering how their actions have affected not only their relationships with others but also their relationship with the spiritual world. Peacemaking often incorporates prayers, ceremonies, and other spiritual practices that help participants connect with their cultural and spiritual heritage.

Reconciliation is a key goal of the Peacemaking process. Rather than seeking to punish the offender, the process focuses on healing the emotional and spiritual wounds caused by the conflict. Offenders are encouraged to take responsibility for their actions, express remorse, and make amends. Victims, in turn, are given the opportunity to express their feelings, receive support from the community, and participate in the process of reconciliation.

The Peacemaking Process

The Navajo Peacemaking process is designed to be flexible and adaptable, allowing it to address a wide range of conflicts and disputes. While the specifics of the process may vary depending on the nature of the conflict, the following steps are common to most Peacemaking sessions.

1. Initiating the Peacemaking Process

Peacemaking can be initiated by any member of the community, including the victim, the offender, or their families. It can also be recommended by the Navajo Nation court system as an alternative to formal legal proceedings. Once the decision is made to pursue Peacemaking, a Peacemaker is selected to guide the process. Peacemakers are usually elders or community leaders who are respected for their wisdom, knowledge of Navajo traditions, and ability to mediate conflicts.

2. Gathering the Participants

The Peacemaker invites all parties involved in the conflict to participate in the Peacemaking session. This includes the victim, the offender, their families, and any other community members who may have been affected by the conflict. The goal is to create a space where all participants feel comfortable sharing their perspectives and working together to resolve the conflict.

3. Facilitating Dialogue and Reflection

During the Peacemaking session, the Peacemaker facilitates dialogue between the participants. The process is informal, and participants are encouraged to speak openly and honestly about their feelings, experiences, and the impact of the conflict. The Peacemaker may share traditional Navajo stories or teachings that relate to the conflict, helping participants reflect on the broader spiritual and cultural implications of their actions.

Unlike adversarial court proceedings, which focus on assigning blame, Peacemaking encourages participants to identify the underlying issues that led to the conflict and work together to find a resolution. The process emphasizes empathy, understanding, and mutual respect, with the goal of promoting healing and reconciliation.

4. Reaching a Resolution

Once the participants have shared their perspectives and reflected on the conflict, they work together to reach a resolution. This may involve the offender making amends, such as offering an apology, performing acts of service, or providing compensation to the victim. The resolution is designed to address the needs of all parties and restore harmony within the community.

The Peacemaker helps facilitate the resolution, ensuring that it reflects Navajo values and promotes long-term healing. Once a resolution is reached, the participants may participate in a closing ceremony or prayer, symbolizing the restoration of Hózhó.

5. Follow-Up and Reintegration

Peacemaking does not end with the resolution of the conflict. The Peacemaker and the community continue to support the victim and the offender as they work to rebuild their relationships and reintegrate into the community. Follow-up meetings may be held to ensure that the resolution is being implemented and that the parties are healing.

This long-term commitment to reconciliation and reintegration sets Navajo Peacemaking apart from punitive justice systems, which often isolate offenders from the community. In contrast, Peacemaking ensures that offenders are given the opportunity to learn from their mistakes, make amends, and contribute positively to the community.

Challenges and Successes of Integrating Peacemaking with Formal Legal Systems

The Navajo Peacemaking system operates within the unique context of the Navajo Nation, which is a sovereign Indigenous nation within the United States. While Peacemaking has been successfully integrated into the Navajo Nation's judicial system, challenges remain in balancing traditional Navajo justice practices with the formal legal requirements of the U.S. legal system.

Challenges

1. Conflicts with Western Legal Norms

One of the main challenges of integrating Peacemaking with formal legal systems is the conflict between the restorative principles of Navajo justice and the punitive nature of Western legal norms. Western courts often prioritize punishment and deterrence, while Navajo Peacemaking focuses on healing and reconciliation. This difference in approach can create tensions when Peacemaking is used as an alternative to formal court proceedings.

2. Recognition by External Legal Systems

While the Navajo Nation has the authority to implement Peacemaking within its own legal system, there are challenges when cases involve external legal systems, such as state or federal courts. External courts may not fully recognize or understand the principles of Peacemaking, making it difficult to incorporate restorative justice practices in cases that cross jurisdictional boundaries.

Successes

1. Cultural Reaffirmation

The formal recognition of Peacemaking within the Navajo Nation's judicial system has been a significant success in preserving and reaffirming Navajo cultural identity. By incorporating traditional justice practices into modern legal frameworks, the Navajo people have been able to maintain their cultural heritage while addressing contemporary legal challenges.

2. Positive Outcomes for Participants

Research on Navajo Peacemaking has shown that participants—both victims and offenders—often experience greater satisfaction with the outcomes of Peacemaking compared to formal legal proceedings. The focus on healing, reconciliation, and community involvement allows for more meaningful resolutions that address the emotional, spiritual, and social needs of all parties.

Conclusion: Navajo Peacemaking as a Model of Restorative Justice

The Navajo Peacemaking system offers a powerful example of how Indigenous restorative justice practices can promote healing, reconciliation, and long-term harmony within communities. By focusing on restoring Hózhó, involving the entire community, and addressing the spiritual dimensions of harm, Peacemaking ensures that justice is not merely about resolving conflicts but about fostering collective well-being.

As Indigenous communities around the world seek to revitalize their legal traditions and assert their right to self-determination, the Navajo Peacemaking system serves as a model for how traditional justice practices can be integrated into modern legal frameworks. Its emphasis on healing, community involvement, and spiritual reflection offers valuable lessons for creating more compassionate and equitable systems of justice.

Case Studies from Indigenous Communities

4.2 Circle Sentencing in First Nations Communities in Canada

Circle sentencing is a prominent example of restorative justice practiced within many First Nations communities in Canada. Rooted in Indigenous traditions of conflict resolution, circle sentencing is a community-based approach that brings together victims, offenders, family members, and community members to address the harm caused by wrongdoing. The goal of circle sentencing is not to punish the offender, but to heal the relationships affected by the offense, restore community harmony, and create a path for the offender to make amends and be reintegrated into the community.

Circle sentencing reflects core principles of Indigenous justice systems, including collective responsibility, respect for relationships, and the interconnectedness of all members of the community. It draws on traditional practices that prioritize dialogue, empathy, and consensus-building to resolve conflicts in a way that benefits everyone involved. In many ways, circle sentencing exemplifies how Indigenous restorative justice can be successfully integrated into contemporary legal systems, offering an alternative to punitive justice models that often fail to address the underlying causes of harm.

This case study explores the origins, process, and outcomes of circle sentencing in First Nations communities in Canada. It highlights how circle sentencing reflects Indigenous values of justice, promotes healing and reconciliation, and offers a more inclusive approach to conflict resolution.

Historical Context of Circle Sentencing

Circle sentencing is based on traditional Indigenous methods of conflict resolution that have been practiced by First Nations communities for centuries. Before the imposition of colonial legal systems, Indigenous peoples in Canada relied on community-based approaches to address disputes and wrongdoing. Justice was understood as a communal process aimed at restoring harmony rather than punishing offenders. Disputes were often resolved through dialogue, negotiation, and consensus, with elders and community leaders playing a central role in facilitating these processes.

With the arrival of European settlers, Indigenous justice systems were marginalized, and colonial legal institutions were imposed on First Nations communities. These colonial systems prioritized retribution and punishment, sidelining Indigenous approaches that emphasized healing and reconciliation. Despite this, many Indigenous communities continued to practice their traditional methods of conflict resolution in informal settings.

In the late 20th century, as part of broader efforts to revitalize Indigenous legal traditions and promote restorative justice, circle sentencing was formally reintroduced into the Canadian legal system. It was first used in 1992 in the Yukon Territory, where a First Nations judge, Barry Stuart, initiated the practice as a response to the failures of the mainstream criminal justice system to address the needs of Indigenous peoples. Since then, circle sentencing has spread to various First Nations communities across Canada, offering a culturally relevant alternative to adversarial court processes.

Key Principles of Circle Sentencing

Circle sentencing is grounded in Indigenous values and principles that prioritize healing, community involvement, and the restoration of relationships. These principles guide the process and outcomes of circle sentencing, ensuring that justice is achieved in a way that reflects the cultural and social values of First Nations communities.

1. Collective Responsibility and Community Involvement

One of the central principles of circle sentencing is the involvement of the entire community in the justice process. Unlike adversarial court systems, where the state assumes responsibility for prosecuting and punishing offenders, circle sentencing emphasizes the collective responsibility of the community to address harm and support both the victim and the offender.

In circle sentencing, community members, including elders, family members, and other respected figures, actively participate in the process. They offer guidance, share their perspectives, and help determine the best way to resolve the conflict. By involving the community, circle sentencing fosters a sense of collective ownership over the justice process, ensuring that the resolution reflects the values and needs of the community as a whole.

2. Restoring Relationships and Healing

The primary goal of circle sentencing is to restore relationships that have been damaged by wrongdoing. In Indigenous worldviews, harm is not just an individual issue; it affects the entire web of relationships within the community. As a result, justice must focus on healing these relationships, rather than simply punishing the offender.

Circle sentencing provides a space for victims to express how the harm has affected them and for offenders to take responsibility for their actions. Through dialogue and mutual understanding, both parties are encouraged to work toward reconciliation. The process often includes symbolic acts of reparation, such as apologies or community service, designed to repair the damage done and restore harmony within the community.

3. Consensus-Based Decision Making

In circle sentencing, decisions about how to resolve the conflict are made through consensus rather than by a judge or legal authority. This reflects the traditional Indigenous approach to decision-making, which emphasizes collaboration, respect for diverse perspectives, and the importance of reaching a solution that is acceptable to everyone involved.

During the circle, participants—victims, offenders, family members, and community members—share their perspectives on the harm that has occurred and propose solutions for moving forward. The group works together to reach a consensus on how the offender can make amends and how the community can support both the victim and the offender in the healing process.

The Circle Sentencing Process

The circle sentencing process is designed to be inclusive, respectful, and healing. It follows a structured but flexible format that allows for open dialogue, reflection, and consensus-building. While the specifics of the process may vary depending on the community and the nature of the offense, the following steps are typically involved in circle sentencing.

1. Initiating the Circle

Circle sentencing is usually initiated after an offender has pleaded guilty or has been found guilty in a court of law. The judge or legal authorities may recommend circle sentencing as an alternative to traditional sentencing, especially in cases involving Indigenous offenders. However, participation in circle sentencing is voluntary, and both the victim and the offender must agree to take part in the process.

Once the decision is made to proceed with circle sentencing, a facilitator—often an elder or respected community leader—is chosen to guide the process. The facilitator is responsible for ensuring that the circle is conducted in a respectful and inclusive manner, and that all participants have the opportunity to speak and be heard.

2. Gathering the Circle

The circle includes the victim, the offender, their families, community members, and, in some cases, legal representatives such as judges, lawyers, or probation officers. The circle may also include elders, spiritual leaders, or other respected figures who can offer guidance and support. The goal is to create a space where all voices are heard and where the focus is on healing and reconciliation.

The physical arrangement of the circle is symbolic of the values of equality and interconnectedness. Participants sit in a circle to emphasize that everyone has an equal voice in the process and that the goal is to work together to restore harmony.

3. Sharing Stories and Perspectives

The circle begins with participants sharing their stories and perspectives on the harm that has occurred. The victim is invited to speak about how the offense has affected them, both emotionally and practically, while the offender is encouraged to take responsibility for their actions and express remorse. Family members and community members also share their perspectives, offering support, insights, and guidance.

Storytelling plays a central role in this phase of the process. By sharing their personal experiences, participants foster empathy and understanding, creating a foundation for healing and reconciliation. Elders or spiritual leaders may share traditional stories or teachings that relate to the conflict, helping participants reflect on the broader social and spiritual implications of the offense.

4. Reaching a Consensus on the Resolution

After all participants have shared their stories, the circle works together to reach a consensus on how the offender can make amends and how the community can support the healing process. This may involve a variety of reparative actions, such as apologies, restitution, community service, or participation in healing ceremonies.

The resolution is designed to address the needs of the victim, the offender, and the community as a whole. It aims to restore relationships, repair the harm caused, and ensure that the offender is reintegrated into the community in a positive and meaningful way.

5. Follow-Up and Accountability

Circle sentencing does not end with the resolution. The community continues to support both the victim and the offender as they implement the agreed-upon reparative actions. Follow-up meetings or check-ins may be scheduled to ensure that the resolution is being carried out and that both parties are healing. This long-term commitment to accountability and support helps prevent recidivism and promotes lasting peace within the community.

Successes and Challenges of Circle Sentencing

Circle sentencing has been widely praised for its ability to promote healing, restore relationships, and reduce recidivism. However, it also faces challenges, particularly when it intersects with the formal legal system or when applied in communities with complex social dynamics.

Successes

1. Healing and Reconciliation

One of the most significant successes of circle sentencing is its ability to promote healing and reconciliation. By providing a space for open dialogue and mutual understanding, circle sentencing helps victims feel heard and supported, while offering offenders the opportunity to take responsibility for their actions and make amends. This process fosters a sense of closure and allows both parties to move forward in peace.

2. Community Involvement

Circle sentencing strengthens community bonds by involving community members in the justice process. The collective responsibility of the community ensures that justice is not only about resolving individual disputes but about maintaining social harmony and supporting the well-being of all members. This involvement also provides a support network for both the victim and the offender, helping them heal and reintegrate into the community.

3. Culturally Relevant Justice

For Indigenous communities, circle sentencing provides a culturally relevant alternative to adversarial court systems. It reflects traditional values of collective responsibility, respect for relationships, and the interconnectedness of all members of the community. By integrating these values into the justice process, circle sentencing helps preserve Indigenous legal traditions while addressing contemporary challenges.

Challenges

1. Integration with Formal Legal Systems

One of the main challenges of circle sentencing is its integration with formal legal systems. While circle sentencing is recognized as a legitimate alternative to traditional sentencing in many parts of Canada, there can be tensions between the restorative principles of circle sentencing and the punitive focus of Western legal systems. Legal authorities may be hesitant to fully embrace circle sentencing, particularly in cases involving serious offenses.

2. Addressing Complex Social Issues

Circle sentencing can be challenging to implement in communities with complex social issues, such as high rates of poverty, addiction, or intergenerational trauma. While the process is designed to promote healing and reconciliation, it may be difficult to address these deeper social problems within the framework of circle sentencing alone. In such cases, additional support services may be needed to address the root causes of harm.

Conclusion: Circle Sentencing as a Model for Restorative Justice

Circle sentencing in First Nations communities in Canada offers a powerful example of how Indigenous restorative justice practices can promote healing, reconciliation, and social harmony. By focusing on repairing relationships, involving the community, and addressing the spiritual and emotional dimensions of harm, circle sentencing provides a holistic and culturally relevant approach to justice.

As Indigenous communities continue to revitalize their legal traditions and assert their right to self-determination, circle sentencing serves as a model for how traditional justice practices can be integrated into contemporary legal frameworks. Its emphasis on collective responsibility, empathy, and healing offers valuable lessons for creating more compassionate and equitable systems of justice, both within Indigenous communities and beyond.

Case Studies from Indigenous Communities

4.3 Māori Approaches to Justice in New Zealand

The Māori people of New Zealand have long maintained distinctive approaches to justice that are deeply rooted in their cultural, spiritual, and social traditions. For the

Māori, justice is not merely about determining guilt or administering punishment but about restoring balance, repairing relationships, and maintaining the well-being of the community. Central to Māori approaches to justice are the concepts of whānau (family), whakawhanaungatanga (building relationships), mana (authority, respect, and dignity), and tapu (sacredness). These values shape a restorative and community-focused approach to conflict resolution.

Traditional Māori justice practices emphasize collective responsibility and seek to repair harm through reconciliation and reintegration rather than isolation or punishment. In recent decades, Māori approaches to justice have gained increasing recognition and have been integrated into New Zealand's formal legal system. Practices such as whānau conferencing and Marae-based justice programs have become prominent examples of how Māori restorative principles can complement and enhance state-run justice systems.

This chapter explores the historical context, principles, and processes of Māori justice practices, focusing on how they exemplify Indigenous restorative justice and their ongoing integration into New Zealand's broader legal framework.

Historical Context of Māori Justice

Before the arrival of European settlers in New Zealand, Māori communities practiced their own systems of governance and justice, grounded in tikanga Māori (Māori customs and laws). Tikanga Māori was—and continues to be—based on maintaining the balance of relationships within and between whānau (families), hapū (subtribes), and iwi (tribes). Justice was traditionally administered by tribal leaders, who acted as mediators and facilitators of reconciliation when conflicts arose. Māori justice was collective, holistic, and centered on restoring harmony rather than simply punishing offenders.

With the colonization of New Zealand in the 19th century, British legal systems were imposed on the Māori people, marginalizing traditional justice practices. The Treaty of Waitangi, signed in 1840 between Māori chiefs and the British Crown, was intended to protect Māori land and sovereignty, but its terms were frequently violated. Māori were increasingly subjected to the colonial justice system, which was adversarial, punitive, and foreign to their values.

Despite this, Māori communities continued to uphold their traditional justice practices in informal settings, particularly within their whānau and on their Marae (meeting grounds). In the late 20th century, efforts to revitalize Māori culture and assert Māori rights led to a renewed focus on integrating Māori justice practices into the formal legal system. This movement aimed to address the disproportionate representation of Māori in the criminal justice system and to create culturally relevant alternatives that aligned with Māori values of reconciliation and collective well-being.

Key Principles of Māori Approaches to Justice

Māori approaches to justice are guided by several key principles that reflect the values of respect, relationships, and collective responsibility. These principles shape the way justice is understood and administered in Māori communities and inform the restorative practices that have been integrated into New Zealand's legal system.

1. Whakapapa and Whānau (Genealogy and Family)

Whakapapa, or genealogy, is a central concept in Māori culture. It refers to the interconnectedness of individuals through their ancestry and their relationships within their whānau, hapū, and iwi. In Māori justice, whakapapa emphasizes that individuals are not isolated beings but are deeply connected to their families and communities. When harm occurs, it affects not only the victim and the offender but also their broader network of relationships.

The concept of whānau is similarly important. Whānau extends beyond the nuclear family to include extended relatives, friends, and even ancestors. In the Māori justice process, the whānau plays a crucial role in resolving conflicts and supporting both the victim and the offender. Māori justice is therefore not an individual matter but a collective responsibility.

2. Mana and Tapu (Authority, Dignity, and Sacredness)

Mana refers to a person's authority, status, and personal dignity. It is a deeply spiritual concept that is closely linked to one's role within the community and one's connection to the ancestors. In Māori justice, preserving the mana of all parties—victim, offender, and community members—is essential. When harm occurs, it diminishes the mana of both the victim and the offender, and the justice process seeks to restore it.

Tapu refers to the sacredness of people, places, and objects. In the context of justice, tapu emphasizes the importance of treating others with respect and acknowledging the spiritual dimensions of harm and healing. The violation of tapu through wrongdoing creates a need for spiritual and emotional restoration, which is often addressed through rituals and ceremonies that help to cleanse and heal those involved.

3. Whakawhanaungatanga (Building and Maintaining Relationships)

Whakawhanaungatanga refers to the process of building and maintaining relationships. In Māori culture, relationships are at the heart of all social interactions, and maintaining these relationships is essential for the well-being of the community. When harm occurs, the focus of justice is on repairing the relationships that have been damaged and ensuring that both the victim and the offender are reintegrated into the community.

Māori justice processes emphasize dialogue, mutual understanding, and collective decision-making as ways to restore relationships and heal the community. This is reflected in practices such as whānau conferencing, where all parties come together to discuss the harm, take responsibility, and work toward reconciliation.

Māori Justice Practices: Whānau Conferencing

One of the most well-known Māori justice practices is whānau conferencing (family group conferencing), a restorative justice process that brings together the victim, the offender, their families, and other community members to address harm and find a resolution. Whānau conferencing is based on Māori values of collective responsibility, respect for relationships, and the importance of reconciliation.

Whānau conferencing was first formally introduced into New Zealand's youth justice system in 1989 with the passage of the Children, Young Persons, and Their Families

Act, which established family group conferences as a central component of the youth justice process. This legislation was designed in part to address the overrepresentation of Māori youth in the criminal justice system and to create a culturally appropriate alternative to traditional court proceedings.

Since its introduction, whānau conferencing has been used in a variety of contexts, including youth justice, adult criminal justice, and child welfare cases. It is widely regarded as a successful model of restorative justice that reflects Māori values while also being accessible to the broader New Zealand population.

The Whānau Conferencing Process

Whānau conferencing typically follows a structured process that allows all participants to share their perspectives and work together to find a resolution. While the specifics of the process may vary depending on the case, the following steps are common to most whānau conferences:

1. Preparation and Engagement

Whānau conferencing begins with the preparation of all participants. This includes discussions with the victim, the offender, and their respective families to ensure that everyone is willing to participate in the process. A trained facilitator, who is often familiar with Māori culture and values, helps guide the participants through the preparation phase, setting expectations and providing support.

2. Gathering the Whānau

The conference itself brings together the victim, the offender, their families, and other relevant parties, such as community elders, social workers, and legal representatives. The goal is to create a space where all participants feel comfortable sharing their experiences and working toward a resolution. The conference is typically held on a Marae, a traditional Māori meeting place, to emphasize the cultural and spiritual significance of the process.

3. Sharing Stories and Perspectives

During the conference, participants are invited to share their perspectives on the harm that has occurred. The victim is given the opportunity to speak first, describing how the offense has affected them and their whānau. The offender is then encouraged to take responsibility for their actions and to express remorse.

Family members and community members also share their views, offering support to both the victim and the offender. This process of storytelling fosters empathy and understanding, creating a foundation for reconciliation.

4. Reaching a Consensus

After all participants have shared their stories, the group works together to reach a consensus on how the offender can make amends and how the community can support the healing process. This may involve a variety of reparative actions, such as apologies, restitution, community service, or participation in healing rituals. The resolution is designed to restore the mana of both the victim and the offender and to repair the relationships that have been damaged.

5. Follow-Up and Reintegration

Whānau conferencing does not end with the resolution. The community continues to support both the victim and the offender as they implement the agreed-upon reparative actions. Follow-up meetings may be held to ensure that the resolution is being carried out and that both parties are healing.

Marae-Based Justice Programs

In addition to whānau conferencing, some Māori communities have developed Marae-based justice programs, which integrate traditional Māori practices into the formal justice system. These programs are held on the Marae, the sacred meeting grounds that are central to Māori cultural and spiritual life. Marae-based programs are designed to address a range of issues, from minor offenses to more serious crimes, and they emphasize the role of the community in supporting both the victim and the offender.

Marae-based justice programs often include elements of Māori spirituality, such as karakia (prayers), pōwhiri (welcome ceremonies), and waiata (songs), which help participants connect with their cultural roots and the spiritual dimensions of justice. The involvement of elders and spiritual leaders ensures that the process is guided by Māori values and that the focus remains on healing and reconciliation.

Challenges and Successes of Māori Justice Practices

Māori justice

practices, including whānau conferencing and Marae-based programs, have been widely praised for their ability to promote healing, restore relationships, and reduce recidivism. However, there are also challenges associated with integrating these practices into New Zealand's formal legal system.

Successes

1. Culturally Relevant Justice

One of the most significant successes of Māori justice practices is their cultural relevance. These practices reflect Māori values of collective responsibility, respect for relationships, and the importance of spiritual and emotional healing. By providing a space for victims, offenders, and their families to come together and work toward reconciliation, Māori justice practices offer a meaningful alternative to adversarial court systems.

2. Reduced Recidivism

Research has shown that Māori justice practices, particularly whānau conferencing, are effective at reducing recidivism. Offenders who participate in whānau conferencing are less likely to reoffend than those who go through traditional court processes. This is largely due to the focus on accountability, reintegration, and community support, which helps offenders address the underlying issues that contributed to their behavior.

3. Strengthening Community Bonds

Māori justice practices emphasize the role of the community in resolving conflicts and supporting both the victim and the offender. This collective approach strengthens social bonds and promotes long-term harmony within the community. By involving the community in the justice process, Māori practices ensure that justice is not just about punishment but about restoring balance and healing relationships.

Challenges

1. Integration with Formal Legal Systems

While Māori justice practices have been integrated into New Zealand's legal system, there are ongoing challenges in ensuring that these practices are fully respected and supported within the broader framework of state-run justice.

Some legal authorities may be hesitant to embrace restorative approaches, particularly in cases involving serious offenses.

2. Addressing Systemic Inequalities

Māori continue to be overrepresented in New Zealand's criminal justice system, a legacy of colonialism and systemic inequality. While Māori justice practices offer a culturally relevant alternative, they cannot fully address the broader social and economic issues that contribute to high rates of Māori incarceration. Addressing these systemic inequalities requires ongoing efforts to promote social justice, economic equity, and cultural revitalization.

Conclusion: Māori Approaches to Justice as a Model for Restorative Practices

Māori approaches to justice offer a powerful model for how Indigenous restorative justice practices can promote healing, reconciliation, and the restoration of relationships. By focusing on collective responsibility, respect for relationships, and the spiritual dimensions of justice, Māori practices provide a culturally relevant alternative to punitive justice systems.

As Indigenous communities continue to revitalize their legal traditions and assert their right to self-determination, Māori justice practices such as whānau conferencing and Marae-based programs serve as examples of how traditional approaches to conflict resolution can be successfully integrated into modern legal frameworks. These practices offer valuable lessons for creating more compassionate, inclusive, and equitable systems of justice, both within New Zealand and beyond.

CHAPTER 05

RESTORATIVE JUSTICE AND MODERN LEGAL SYSTEM

5.1 Challenges and Opportunities in the Application of Indigenous Practices

As the world becomes increasingly aware of the limitations of punitive justice systems, there has been a growing interest in integrating Indigenous restorative justice practices into modern legal frameworks. Indigenous practices, such as circle sentencing, peacemaking, and whānau conferencing, offer valuable insights into how justice can be approached in ways that prioritize healing, reconciliation, and community well-being over punishment and isolation. However, the application of Indigenous practices within modern legal systems is not without its challenges. Issues such as legal legitimacy, cultural appropriation, and the tension between restorative and retributive justice raise important questions about how best to integrate these approaches.

Despite these challenges, there are also significant opportunities. Indigenous practices can provide a model for addressing the failings of punitive systems, particularly in reducing recidivism, promoting long-term community harmony, and addressing the disproportionate incarceration of Indigenous and marginalized peoples. This chapter explores the challenges and opportunities of applying Indigenous restorative justice practices within modern legal systems, examining how these approaches can contribute to a more compassionate and effective model of justice.

Challenges in Applying Indigenous Practices in Modern Legal Systems

Integrating Indigenous restorative justice practices into state-run legal systems presents several challenges, particularly when these systems are built on different philosophical foundations. The Western legal tradition, which tends to prioritize individual rights, punishment, and deterrence, often conflicts with Indigenous practices that emphasize community responsibility, healing, and reconciliation. These differences can create obstacles in the application of Indigenous practices within formal legal structures.

1. Legal Legitimacy and Recognition

One of the primary challenges in applying Indigenous restorative justice practices within modern legal systems is the issue of legal legitimacy and recognition. In many countries, state-run legal systems have long marginalized or suppressed Indigenous justice practices, viewing them as informal, primitive, or incompatible with the rule of law. This legacy of colonialism has resulted in a legal framework that often fails to recognize the legitimacy of Indigenous justice systems.

For example, while practices like circle sentencing and whānau conferencing have been integrated into some formal legal frameworks, they are often seen as supplementary to, rather than on equal footing with, state-run courts and legal procedures. In some cases, the involvement of Indigenous practices in the justice process is only permitted as an alternative form of sentencing after the offender has already been found guilty in a court of law. This limits the full application of Indigenous justice principles and reduces the role of community-based decision-making.

The challenge, then, is how to ensure that Indigenous restorative justice practices are given equal recognition and authority within modern legal systems. This requires a shift in perspective, one that values the contributions of Indigenous legal traditions and recognizes them as legitimate and effective approaches to justice.

2. Cultural Appropriation and Misrepresentation

Another significant challenge is the risk of cultural appropriation and misrepresentation of Indigenous justice practices when they are adopted into modern legal systems. Indigenous justice is deeply rooted in the cultural, spiritual, and social values of specific communities. It is not simply a set of techniques or procedures that can be transplanted into another context without considering the cultural framework that gives them meaning.

In some cases, elements of Indigenous restorative justice, such as circle sentencing or peacemaking, have been incorporated into non-Indigenous legal systems in ways that strip them of their cultural significance. When these practices are used without the involvement of Indigenous leaders, elders, or communities, there is a risk that they will be misrepresented or reduced to mere tools of alternative dispute resolution, divorced from their deeper spiritual and cultural roots.

Ensuring that Indigenous justice practices are applied in a culturally respectful and meaningful way requires the involvement of Indigenous communities at every stage of the process. This includes recognizing the authority of

Indigenous elders and leaders, incorporating spiritual and cultural elements into the justice process, and ensuring that practices are not used in ways that undermine their original intent.

3. Balancing Restorative and Retributive Justice

A third challenge in applying Indigenous restorative justice practices within modern legal systems is the tension between restorative and retributive approaches to justice. Modern legal systems, particularly in Western countries, have traditionally emphasized retribution, punishment, and deterrence as the primary goals of justice. This focus on punishment often conflicts with the principles of Indigenous restorative justice, which prioritize healing, reconciliation, and the restoration of relationships.

In cases involving serious crimes, such as violence or sexual assault, there can be resistance to the idea of using restorative justice practices, which are sometimes perceived as too lenient. Critics argue that restorative justice may not provide sufficient punishment or deterrence for serious offenses, and that it could result in a failure to adequately protect victims or the broader public.

Balancing these two approaches requires a nuanced understanding of both restorative and retributive justice. While restorative justice may not be appropriate in every case, it can be highly effective in addressing certain types of harm, particularly those that involve ongoing relationships within a community. Modern legal systems must find ways to incorporate restorative practices without abandoning their responsibility to ensure accountability and public safety.

Opportunities for Integrating Indigenous Restorative Justice Practices

Despite the challenges, there are significant opportunities for integrating Indigenous restorative justice practices into modern legal systems. These practices offer a model for addressing some of the most pressing issues in contemporary justice systems, including high rates of recidivism, the overrepresentation of Indigenous peoples in prisons, and the need for more compassionate and effective responses to harm.

1. Reducing Recidivism and Promoting Rehabilitation

One of the most well-documented benefits of Indigenous restorative justice practices is their ability to reduce recidivism and promote the rehabilitation of offenders. Research has shown that offenders who participate in restorative justice programs are less likely to reoffend than those who go through traditional court systems. This is largely because restorative justice focuses on accountability, personal growth, and reintegration, rather than punishment and isolation.

Indigenous justice practices such as circle sentencing and whānau conferencing provide offenders with the opportunity to take responsibility for their actions, make amends to the victim, and work toward reconciliation with the community. These processes promote personal reflection and growth, helping offenders understand the broader impact of their actions and encouraging them to make positive changes in their lives. By focusing on rehabilitation rather than retribution, Indigenous justice practices help break the cycle of reoffending and create opportunities for offenders to contribute positively to society.

2. Addressing the Overrepresentation of Indigenous Peoples in the Criminal Justice System

Indigenous peoples are disproportionately represented in the criminal justice systems of many countries, including Canada, Australia, New Zealand, and the United States. This overrepresentation is often the result of historical injustices, systemic racism, and social and economic marginalization. Indigenous justice practices offer an alternative approach that can help address this disparity by providing culturally relevant and community-based alternatives to incarceration.

By incorporating Indigenous restorative justice practices into modern legal systems, governments can create pathways for Indigenous offenders to participate in justice processes that reflect their cultural values and address the root causes of their behavior. This not only helps reduce the overrepresentation of Indigenous peoples in prisons but also promotes healing and reconciliation within Indigenous communities.

In countries like Canada, for example, the use of circle sentencing and other Indigenous justice practices has been shown to significantly reduce the likelihood of reoffending among Indigenous offenders. These practices provide a more culturally appropriate response to harm, helping to address the broader social and historical context that contributes to criminal behavior.

3. Strengthening Community Bonds and Promoting Social Harmony

Indigenous restorative justice practices offer a unique opportunity to strengthen community bonds and promote long-term social harmony. By involving the entire community in the justice process, these practices foster a sense of collective responsibility and encourage individuals to take an active role in supporting both the victim and the offender. This approach not only helps repair relationships but also creates a stronger, more resilient community.

In contrast to punitive justice systems, which often isolate offenders from their communities, Indigenous justice practices emphasize reintegration and reconciliation. Offenders are given the opportunity to make amends and rebuild trust with their families and communities, while victims receive the support they need to heal from the harm they have experienced. This collective approach to justice helps prevent future conflict and creates a foundation for long-term peace and stability.

4. Offering a Model for Restorative Justice Reform

Indigenous justice practices provide a valuable model for restorative justice reform in modern legal systems. As more governments recognize the limitations of punitive justice, there is growing interest in developing alternatives that promote healing, accountability, and community involvement. Indigenous practices offer a well-established framework for how restorative justice can be implemented in a way that addresses both the needs of victims and the broader community.

Incorporating Indigenous principles of justice—such as collective responsibility, reconciliation, and the restoration of relationships—into modern legal systems can help create more compassionate and effective responses to harm. These principles offer a path toward justice that prioritizes healing over punishment and recognizes the importance of addressing the root causes of conflict.

Conclusion: The Path Forward for Integrating Indigenous Restorative Justice

The integration of Indigenous restorative justice practices into modern legal systems presents both challenges and opportunities. While issues of legal legitimacy, cultural appropriation, and the tension between restorative and retributive justice must be carefully navigated, there is significant potential for these practices to transform how justice is understood and administered.

By focusing on healing, accountability, and community well-being, Indigenous restorative justice practices offer a more holistic and compassionate approach to justice. They provide a model for addressing the failings of punitive systems, particularly in reducing recidivism, promoting social harmony, and addressing the overrepresentation of Indigenous peoples in prisons.

As governments and legal systems seek to reform justice processes and create more equitable outcomes, Indigenous restorative justice practices offer valuable lessons for creating a more just, inclusive, and healing-oriented society. The path forward requires a commitment to recognizing the legitimacy of Indigenous legal traditions, ensuring cultural integrity in the application of these practices, and balancing restorative and retributive approaches to justice. By doing so, we can create a more compassionate and effective model of justice for all.

Restorative Justice and Modern Legal Systems

5.2 Interaction with Formal Justice Systems

As Indigenous restorative justice practices gain recognition and are increasingly applied in contemporary legal contexts, their interaction with formal justice systems presents both challenges and opportunities. Formal justice systems, particularly in Western contexts, are based on legal frameworks that prioritize individual rights, legal procedure, and punitive outcomes, whereas Indigenous justice practices are rooted in collective responsibility, healing, and the restoration of social harmony. The convergence of these two systems raises questions about compatibility, cultural integrity, and how best to integrate these distinct approaches to justice.

In this section, we explore how Indigenous restorative justice practices interact with formal justice systems. We examine the ways in which these practices have been incorporated into state-run legal systems, the challenges of maintaining the cultural and philosophical integrity of

Indigenous approaches, and the potential benefits of integrating restorative principles into formal justice processes.

1. Incorporation of Indigenous Practices into Formal Justice Systems

Over the past few decades, there has been growing recognition of the value of Indigenous restorative justice practices, and efforts have been made to incorporate these approaches into formal justice systems. This integration has been driven in part by the failure of punitive justice models to reduce recidivism or address the root causes of crime, as well as by the desire to offer culturally relevant alternatives for Indigenous communities disproportionately impacted by the criminal justice system.

Several countries, including Canada, New Zealand, and Australia, have introduced programs that incorporate Indigenous restorative justice practices into their formal legal frameworks. These initiatives often focus on youth justice, sentencing alternatives, and community-based conflict resolution. In these cases, Indigenous practices such as circle sentencing, whānau conferencing, and peacemaking have been adapted to work alongside traditional court systems.

Examples of Incorporation

- Canada: Circle Sentencing and Gladue Courts

In Canada, the use of circle sentencing has been formally integrated into the criminal justice system as an alternative to traditional sentencing, particularly for Indigenous offenders. Circle sentencing brings together the victim, the offender, their families, and community members to discuss the harm caused and agree on an appropriate resolution. This process is grounded in Indigenous values of reconciliation, healing, and collective responsibility.

In addition to circle sentencing, Canada has established Gladue courts, which focus on applying restorative justice principles to cases involving Indigenous offenders. Gladue courts are based on the 1999 Supreme Court ruling in R v Gladue, which recognized the need for courts to consider the unique circumstances of Indigenous offenders and apply culturally relevant alternatives to incarceration. These courts incorporate Indigenous perspectives and practices into the legal process, offering an alternative to traditional sentencing approaches.

- New Zealand: Whānau Conferencing

In New Zealand, whānau conferencing (family group conferencing) has been formally integrated into the youth justice system since the passage of the Children, Young Persons, and Their Families Act in 1989. Whānau conferencing allows the victim, the offender, their families, and community members to come together to discuss the harm caused and determine an appropriate resolution. This process reflects Māori values of collective responsibility and the importance of repairing relationships within the community.

The success of whānau conferencing has led to its expansion into other areas of the justice system, including adult criminal justice and child welfare cases. It has been widely recognized as an effective model for reducing recidivism and promoting healing within Māori communities.

- Australia: Indigenous Sentencing Courts

In Australia, Indigenous sentencing courts have been established as part of an effort to address the overrepresentation of Indigenous Australians in the criminal justice system. These courts, such as the Koori Court in Victoria and the Murri Court in Queensland, incorporate Indigenous practices such as circle sentencing and involve elders and community leaders in the sentencing process. These courts focus on rehabilitation, reintegration, and culturally appropriate sentencing options for Indigenous offenders.

2. Challenges in the Interaction between Indigenous and Formal Justice Systems

While the incorporation of Indigenous restorative justice practices into formal legal frameworks has led to positive outcomes in many cases, there are also significant challenges. These challenges include the potential for cultural dilution, the difficulty of balancing restorative and punitive approaches, and the need for ongoing community involvement.

Cultural Dilution and Misrepresentation

One of the major challenges in the interaction between Indigenous and formal justice systems is the risk of cultural dilution. When Indigenous restorative justice practices are incorporated into state-run legal systems, there is a risk that they will be altered or simplified in ways that strip them of their cultural and spiritual significance. For example, practices such as circle sentencing may be reduced to a procedural alternative to traditional court proceedings, without fully incorporating the values of collective responsibility, spiritual healing, and reconciliation that are central to Indigenous justice.

In some cases, the involvement of elders, spiritual leaders, and community members may be limited, reducing the depth and effectiveness of the restorative process. Additionally, formal justice systems may prioritize efficiency and legal outcomes over the more holistic, relationship-focused approach that is at the heart of Indigenous justice practices.

To address this challenge, it is essential that Indigenous communities are fully involved in the design and implementation of restorative justice programs. Elders and community leaders must be given the authority to guide the process, ensuring that the practices remain true to their cultural origins and maintain their focus on healing and reconciliation.

Tension between Restorative and Retributive Justice

Another challenge is the tension between restorative justice and retributive justice. Formal legal systems are often based on retributive principles, which prioritize punishment and deterrence. These systems may view restorative justice practices as too lenient, particularly in cases involving serious offenses. As a result, there can be resistance to fully embracing restorative justice approaches, especially when they are seen as incompatible with the goals of public safety and accountability.

For example, in cases involving violent crimes, there may be concerns that restorative justice practices do not provide sufficient punishment or protection for the victim. In such cases, courts may be hesitant to use restorative justice as the primary means of addressing harm, preferring instead to impose more punitive measures such as incarceration.

Balancing restorative and retributive approaches requires a careful consideration of the goals of justice. While restorative justice may not be appropriate in every case, it can be highly effective in addressing certain types of harm, particularly when there is an ongoing relationship between the victim and the offender. Modern legal systems must find ways to incorporate restorative principles without undermining their responsibility to ensure accountability and public safety.

Community Involvement and Capacity

Indigenous restorative justice practices rely heavily on the involvement of the community, including elders, family members, and other community leaders. However, in some cases, there may be challenges related to the capacity of communities to fully participate in the justice process. This can be particularly true in communities that have experienced significant social and economic marginalization, where there may be limited resources to support restorative justice initiatives.

For example, in some Indigenous communities, there may be a shortage of elders or spiritual leaders who are able to guide the justice process. Additionally, the involvement of the broader community may be difficult in cases where social bonds have been weakened by factors such as poverty, substance abuse, or intergenerational trauma.

Addressing these challenges requires a commitment to strengthening community capacity and providing the necessary resources to support Indigenous justice practices. This may include training programs for elders and community leaders, as well as funding for restorative justice programs that are culturally appropriate and community-driven.

3. Opportunities for Integrating Restorative Principles into Formal Justice Systems

Despite the challenges, the interaction between Indigenous restorative justice practices and formal justice systems presents significant opportunities for reform. As governments and legal systems recognize the limitations of punitive justice, Indigenous practices offer valuable lessons for creating more compassionate, inclusive, and effective responses to harm.

Reducing Overrepresentation of Indigenous Peoples in Prisons

One of the most significant opportunities is the potential for Indigenous restorative justice practices to help reduce the overrepresentation of Indigenous peoples in prisons. In many countries, Indigenous peoples are incarcerated at disproportionately high rates, often due to systemic racism, social inequality, and the legacy of colonization. Restorative justice practices that focus on rehabilitation, reconciliation, and reintegration offer a promising alternative to incarceration, particularly for low-level offenses.

By providing culturally relevant alternatives to imprisonment, Indigenous justice practices can help break the cycle of incarceration and promote healing within Indigenous communities. This, in turn, can contribute to broader efforts to address the social and economic factors that contribute to criminal behavior.

Promoting Long-Term Healing and Reconciliation

Indigenous restorative justice practices are uniquely positioned to promote long-term healing and reconciliation, both within communities and within the broader society. Unlike punitive justice systems, which often leave both victims and offenders disconnected from the justice process, restorative practices focus on repairing relationships and restoring social harmony. This approach is particularly important in cases involving ongoing relationships, such as those within families or small communities.

By incorporating restorative principles into formal justice systems, governments can create pathways for victims and offenders to engage in meaningful dialogue, take responsibility for their actions, and work toward reconciliation. This not only benefits the individuals involved but also contributes to long-term social cohesion and peace.

Inspiring Broader Justice Reform

The integration of Indigenous restorative justice practices into formal legal systems offers a model for broader justice reform. As punitive approaches to justice continue to face criticism for their failure to reduce recidivism or address the root causes of crime, restorative justice provides a promising alternative that prioritizes healing, accountability, and community involvement.

Indigenous practices such as circle sentencing, whānau conferencing, and peacemaking offer valuable insights into how justice can be reimagined in ways that promote both individual and collective well-being. By learning from these practices, modern legal systems can develop more compassionate and effective responses to harm, creating a justice system that is truly focused on restoration and healing.

Conclusion: Navigating the Interaction Between Indigenous and Formal Justice Systems

The interaction between Indigenous restorative justice practices and formal justice systems presents both challenges and opportunities. While there are obstacles related to legal legitimacy, cultural integrity, and the tension between restorative and retributive justice, there is also significant potential for Indigenous practices to transform how justice is understood and administered.

By incorporating Indigenous restorative justice practices into modern legal systems, governments can address the shortcomings of punitive justice models, reduce the overrepresentation of Indigenous peoples in prisons, and promote long-term healing and reconciliation within communities. However, this requires a commitment to ensuring that Indigenous practices are applied in culturally respectful and meaningful ways, with the full involvement of Indigenous communities at every stage of the process.

As we move forward, the lessons of Indigenous justice offer a powerful model for creating a more compassionate, inclusive, and restorative justice system for all.

Restorative Justice and Modern Legal Systems

5.3 Creating Synergies Between Western and Indigenous Justice

The convergence of Western legal systems and Indigenous restorative justice practices offers the potential to create a more holistic, inclusive, and effective approach to justice. Western legal systems, typically grounded in retributive justice, prioritize individual rights, legal formalism, and punishment, while Indigenous justice systems are centered on collective responsibility, reconciliation, and healing. Although these two systems have historically been seen as incompatible, there is growing recognition that they can complement each other to create a more just society.

Creating synergies between Western and Indigenous justice requires mutual respect, a commitment to understanding the values that underpin each system, and a willingness to integrate the best elements of both. This chapter explores how the strengths of Western and Indigenous justice can be harmonized, addressing the opportunities and challenges of blending these approaches to develop a justice system that promotes healing, accountability, and social harmony.

1. Understanding the Complementary Strengths of Western and Indigenous Justice

The Western and Indigenous approaches to justice each offer valuable strengths that, when combined, can address the limitations of purely retributive or purely restorative models. By acknowledging and building on these strengths, it is possible to create a justice system that addresses the needs of both individuals and communities.

1.1 Strengths of Western Justice

Western legal systems, particularly those based on common law or civil law traditions, have developed rigorous procedures and institutions that ensure fairness, consistency, and the protection of individual rights. Some of the key strengths of Western justice include:

- Legal formalism and procedural consistency: Western justice systems are characterized by their formal structures, legal procedures, and rules of evidence. This ensures that justice is administered consistently and that legal outcomes are predictable and based on established legal principles.

- Protection of individual rights: Western justice systems prioritize the protection of individual rights, including the right to a fair trial, legal representation, and due process. These protections help prevent the abuse of power and ensure that all individuals are treated equally before the law.

- Accountability and deterrence: The retributive focus of Western justice serves as a mechanism for holding individuals accountable for their actions and deterring future crimes. Punishment, in the form of fines, incarceration, or other penalties, is seen as a way to maintain public order and discourage criminal behavior.

1.2 Strengths of Indigenous Justice

Indigenous justice systems, which are deeply rooted in the cultural and spiritual values of Indigenous peoples, emphasize reconciliation, healing, and the restoration of relationships. Key strengths of Indigenous justice include:

- Collective responsibility and community involvement: Indigenous justice practices view harm as something that affects not only the individual but the entire community. As a result, the justice process involves the collective participation of the community in addressing the harm, supporting both the victim and the offender, and ensuring that social harmony is restored.

- Focus on healing and reconciliation: Rather than prioritizing punishment, Indigenous justice seeks to heal the emotional, psychological, and spiritual wounds caused by harm. This approach helps both the victim and the offender achieve closure and promotes long-term peace and well-being within the community.

- Restorative justice principles: Indigenous justice is inherently restorative, focusing on repairing the damage caused by wrongdoing, making amends, and reintegrating the offender into the community. This approach reduces the likelihood of recidivism and fosters a culture of mutual respect and responsibility.

2. Opportunities for Creating Synergies

There are numerous opportunities to create synergies between Western and Indigenous justice by integrating the strengths of both systems into a cohesive and balanced approach. This integration can take place at multiple levels, including procedural innovations, community-based justice initiatives, and legal reforms that recognize the value of restorative justice.

2.1 Integrating Restorative Justice into Sentencing and Rehabilitation

One of the most promising opportunities for creating synergies is the integration of restorative justice practices into sentencing and rehabilitation processes within Western legal systems. Many countries, including Canada, New Zealand, and Australia, have already begun to incorporate Indigenous restorative justice practices such as circle sentencing, whānau conferencing, and peacemaking into their formal legal frameworks.

By offering restorative justice options alongside traditional sentencing, Western courts can provide victims, offenders, and communities with a more flexible and compassionate approach to justice. This integration allows for the use of restorative principles in cases where healing and reconciliation are prioritized, while still ensuring that legal protections and accountability mechanisms are in place.

For example, a judge in a Western court might offer an offender the option to participate in a restorative justice circle as part of their sentencing. This process would allow the offender to take responsibility for their actions, make amends to the victim, and work toward reintegration into the community, all while maintaining the legal formalities of the court system.

2.2 Strengthening Community-Based Justice Programs

Another opportunity for synergy lies in the development of community-based justice programs that draw on both Indigenous and Western approaches to justice. These programs can be designed to address the unique needs of specific communities, particularly those with high rates of crime, poverty, or social marginalization.

By empowering local communities to take an active role in the justice process, these programs promote collective responsibility and accountability. Indigenous justice practices can be integrated into these initiatives, providing a culturally relevant framework for resolving conflicts and promoting social harmony. At the same time, the formal legal protections and oversight of Western systems can ensure that these programs are conducted fairly and consistently.

One example of such a synergy is the Gladue courts in Canada, which apply restorative justice principles to cases involving Indigenous offenders. These courts operate within the formal legal system but emphasize community involvement, cultural sensitivity, and restorative outcomes. Similarly, Marae-based justice programs in New Zealand combine Māori cultural practices with formal legal processes to promote healing and reconciliation within Māori communities.

2.3 Legal Reforms to Recognize Indigenous Justice Systems

Creating meaningful synergies between Western and Indigenous justice also requires legal reforms that recognize the legitimacy and authority of Indigenous justice systems. In many countries, Indigenous justice practices have historically been marginalized or excluded from formal legal frameworks. By formally recognizing these practices, governments can create a more inclusive justice system that respects the rights and traditions of Indigenous peoples.

Legal reforms can take various forms, from incorporating Indigenous justice principles into state-run courts to granting Indigenous communities greater autonomy to manage their own justice processes. For example, in Canada, the recognition of Gladue principles requires courts to consider the unique circumstances of Indigenous offenders and apply culturally relevant alternatives to traditional sentencing. Similarly, in Australia, Indigenous sentencing courts operate within the formal legal system but give elders and community leaders a central role in the sentencing process.

3. Challenges in Creating Synergies

While there are many opportunities to create synergies between Western and Indigenous justice, there are also significant challenges that must be addressed. These challenges include maintaining the cultural integrity of Indigenous practices, balancing restorative and punitive approaches, and ensuring that legal systems are flexible enough to accommodate diverse approaches to justice.

3.1 Preserving the Cultural Integrity of Indigenous Practices

One of the primary challenges in creating synergies between Western and Indigenous justice is ensuring that Indigenous practices are not co-opted or diluted when they are integrated into formal legal systems. Indigenous justice is deeply rooted in the cultural, spiritual, and social values of Indigenous communities, and it is essential that these practices retain their integrity and meaning.

To address this challenge, it is crucial that Indigenous communities have full control over the design and implementation of restorative justice programs. Elders, spiritual leaders, and community members must play a central role in guiding the process and ensuring that it remains true to its cultural origins. Governments and legal systems must respect the authority of Indigenous leaders and work collaboratively to create justice programs that reflect Indigenous values.

3.2 Balancing Restorative and Retributive Approaches

Another challenge is finding the right balance between restorative and retributive approaches to justice. While restorative justice is highly effective in addressing certain types of harm, there are cases—such as those involving serious violence or sexual assault—where the public may demand punitive measures to ensure accountability and public safety.

Finding this balance requires a nuanced understanding of the goals of justice. In some cases, a hybrid approach may be appropriate, where restorative justice processes are used alongside traditional sentencing to promote healing while also ensuring that offenders are held accountable for their actions. By combining the strengths of both approaches, it is possible to create a justice system that is both compassionate and effective.

3.3 Flexibility and Adaptability of Legal Systems

Western legal systems are often highly formalized and rigid, making it difficult to integrate alternative approaches such as Indigenous restorative justice. For synergies to be created, legal systems must become more flexible and adaptable, allowing for the incorporation of diverse approaches to justice that reflect the values and needs of different communities.

This flexibility can be achieved through legal reforms that allow for greater discretion in sentencing, the use of alternative dispute resolution mechanisms, and the recognition of community-based justice programs. Courts and legal professionals must also be open to learning from Indigenous practices and willing to experiment with new models of justice that prioritize healing, reconciliation, and social harmony.

4. The Path Forward: Building a Hybrid Justice System

The future of justice lies in the development of hybrid systems that combine the best elements of Western and Indigenous justice. By creating synergies between these two approaches, it is possible to build a justice system that is more inclusive, compassionate, and effective at promoting healing and reconciliation.

Hybrid justice systems would draw on the strengths of Western legal procedures, such as the protection of individual rights and legal formalism, while incorporating the restorative principles of Indigenous justice, such as collective responsibility, community involvement, and healing. These systems would be flexible enough to accommodate diverse approaches to justice, recognizing that different cases and communities may require different solutions.

Building a hybrid justice system will require ongoing collaboration between governments, legal professionals, and Indigenous communities. It will also require a commitment to learning from the strengths of both Western and Indigenous traditions, recognizing that each approach has valuable contributions to make.

Conclusion: A New Vision for Justice

Creating synergies between Western and Indigenous justice offers an exciting opportunity to reimagine how justice is understood and administered. By integrating the strengths of both systems, it is possible to develop a more compassionate, inclusive, and effective approach to justice that promotes healing, accountability, and social harmony.

The path forward involves recognizing the legitimacy and authority of Indigenous justice practices, empowering communities to take an active role in the justice process, and creating legal systems that are flexible enough to accommodate diverse approaches to resolving harm. As governments and legal professionals continue to explore these synergies, they will contribute to the development of a justice system that is truly focused on restoration, reconciliation, and long-term peace.

CHAPTER 06

RESTORATIVE JUSTICE IN THE CONTEXT RECONCILIATION

6.1 Truth and Reconciliation Commissions

Truth and Reconciliation Commissions (TRCs) are processes established to address systemic injustices and human rights violations, particularly those rooted in historical and ongoing colonialism, conflict, and discrimination. These commissions serve as mechanisms for acknowledging past harms, fostering dialogue between affected communities and the state, and charting a path toward healing and reconciliation. TRCs are inherently tied to restorative justice because they focus on restoring relationships, addressing historical wrongs, and promoting healing for both victims and the broader society.

The framework of TRCs emphasizes restorative justice principles, such as the importance of truth-telling, accountability, and reparative action, rather than retribution. They aim to address systemic violence and injustice by giving voice to survivors, acknowledging the harm caused, and identifying ways to repair the damage done. In this chapter, we will explore the role of Truth and Reconciliation Commissions in the context of Indigenous communities and their intersection with restorative justice.

1. Origins and Purpose of Truth and Reconciliation Commissions

Truth and Reconciliation Commissions have been established in many countries worldwide, particularly in post-conflict or post-colonial societies, to address the legacy of large-scale human rights abuses. They originated from the need to address deep-seated societal grievances and to reconcile historically marginalized or oppressed groups with the state or the broader public. TRCs often emerge in contexts where criminal justice systems are unable or unwilling to fully address past atrocities, or where punitive approaches may exacerbate tensions and hinder national unity.

The first widely recognized TRC was established in South Africa in 1995 following the end of apartheid. The South African TRC provided a platform for victims of apartheid-era human rights abuses to share their stories, while also offering amnesty to perpetrators who fully disclosed their involvement in these abuses. The commission sought to promote healing through truth-telling, recognizing that without the acknowledgment of past harms, true reconciliation could not occur.

Following South Africa's example, other countries—including Canada, Sierra Leone, Peru, and Chile—established TRCs to address historical injustices, particularly those related to colonization, ethnic conflict, or dictatorship. In these contexts, TRCs were seen as an alternative to traditional criminal justice, with a focus on restorative principles, such as reconciliation, reparations, and the rebuilding of trust between communities and the state.

2. The Role of Truth in Reconciliation

One of the core functions of TRCs is to establish the truth about historical injustices and atrocities. Truth-telling is critical to the process of reconciliation because it creates a shared understanding of what happened, who was responsible, and how the harm impacted individuals and communities. The act of truth-telling allows survivors to reclaim their narratives, share their pain, and demand accountability for the suffering they endured.

In Indigenous contexts, truth-telling is often essential to addressing the ongoing impacts of colonialism, land dispossession, and cultural suppression. For many Indigenous peoples, the truth of their history has been erased or distorted by dominant narratives that minimize or justify colonial violence. TRCs provide a space for Indigenous voices to be heard and for the broader society to confront uncomfortable truths about its history.

2.1 Truth-Telling and Survivor Testimonies

In TRCs, survivor testimonies play a central role in the truth-telling process. Survivors of human rights violations or historical injustice are invited to share their stories, often in public hearings or written submissions. These testimonies provide powerful personal accounts of the harm experienced and allow survivors to articulate their need for justice and healing.

For example, in the Canadian Truth and Reconciliation Commission (2008–2015), established to address the legacy of the Indian Residential Schools, survivors of the residential school system shared their experiences of abuse, neglect, and cultural loss. These testimonies were vital in raising public awareness about the widespread and systemic nature of the abuses inflicted on Indigenous children and communities over several generations. Truth-telling in this context was not only about documenting history but also about validating the experiences of survivors and recognizing the long-term impacts of these policies on Indigenous peoples.

2.2 Public Acknowledgment and Collective Truth

Beyond individual testimonies, TRCs aim to establish a collective truth about the historical injustices in question. This involves the careful documentation and examination of evidence, including government records, witness statements, and expert analysis. The collective truth serves as a foundation for public acknowledgment of harm, ensuring that these events are officially recognized and memorialized.

In Indigenous contexts, establishing a collective truth is crucial for challenging colonial narratives that have denied or downplayed the harm inflicted on Indigenous peoples. Public acknowledgment of this truth allows for a national reckoning with the past and lays the groundwork for meaningful reconciliation. It also opens the door for further action, such as reparations, policy changes, and legal reforms that address the root causes of systemic injustice.

3. Reconciliation and Restorative Justice

Reconciliation is the ultimate goal of TRCs, but it is not a simple or linear process. Reconciliation requires more than just the acknowledgment of harm; it demands active efforts to repair relationships, restore trust, and ensure that similar harms are not repeated. Restorative justice plays a critical role in this process, as it provides a framework for addressing the needs of survivors, promoting healing, and facilitating accountability.

3.1 Healing and Reparations

In the context of restorative justice, healing is central to reconciliation. TRCs aim to provide survivors with an opportunity to heal by offering a platform for their voices to be heard, their experiences to be validated, and their suffering to be recognized. This healing process often involves symbolic acts of acknowledgment, such as public apologies, memorials, and truth-telling ceremonies, as well as more tangible forms of reparations, including financial compensation, land restitution, and social services.

For example, the Canadian Truth and Reconciliation Commission recommended a series of reparative measures, including financial compensation for survivors of residential schools, support for Indigenous languages and cultures, and legal reforms to address systemic racism and inequality. These reparations are essential to the process of healing and restoring the dignity of those who were harmed.

3.2 *Restoring Relationships and Accountability*

A key aspect of restorative justice is the focus on restoring relationships. TRCs provide a space for dialogue between survivors, perpetrators, and the broader society, with the goal of rebuilding trust and fostering mutual understanding. This relational aspect of reconciliation is particularly important in Indigenous contexts, where harm has often disrupted not only individual lives but also entire communities and cultural systems.

Accountability is also an important element of the reconciliation process. While TRCs often prioritize healing over punishment, they still seek to hold perpetrators accountable for their actions. This accountability may take the form of public acknowledgment, apology, or participation in reparative actions. In some cases, TRCs may work alongside formal justice systems to ensure that perpetrators are held legally accountable, while still promoting restorative outcomes.

For example, in South Africa's TRC, perpetrators who provided full disclosure of their involvement in apartheid-era crimes were granted amnesty, but those who refused to participate or were found guilty of gross human rights violations were subject to prosecution. This balance between truth-telling, accountability, and restorative justice allowed the TRC to facilitate reconciliation while addressing the need for justice.

4. Indigenous Truth and Reconciliation Commissions

Indigenous peoples have played a significant role in the development and implementation of TRCs, particularly in countries with histories of colonialism and systemic discrimination against Indigenous communities. These TRCs have provided a platform for Indigenous voices to be heard and have highlighted the importance of Indigenous perspectives in the broader conversation about reconciliation.

4.1 Canadian Truth and Reconciliation Commission

One of the most significant TRCs focused on Indigenous issues was Canada's Truth and Reconciliation Commission (2008–2015), which was established as part of the Indian Residential Schools Settlement Agreement. The commission was tasked with documenting the experiences of survivors of the residential school system, where Indigenous children were forcibly removed from their families, placed in church-run institutions, and subjected to cultural assimilation, abuse, and neglect.

The Canadian TRC held public hearings across the country, where thousands of survivors shared their stories. The commission's final report, released in 2015, contained 94 Calls to Action, outlining specific steps that governments, institutions, and the public could take to address the legacy of residential schools and promote reconciliation with Indigenous peoples.

The Canadian TRC highlighted the central role of Indigenous worldviews in the reconciliation process, emphasizing the importance of spirituality, land, and cultural restoration. Its work also led to significant policy changes, including the creation of the National Centre for Truth and Reconciliation, the implementation of Indigenous language revitalization programs, and the formal apology from the Canadian government to residential school survivors.

4.2 Australian Truth and Reconciliation Efforts

In Australia, efforts to address the legacy of colonialism and the Stolen Generations—Indigenous children forcibly removed from their families under government policies—have also involved truth-telling and reconciliation initiatives. The Bringing Them Home report

(1997), which documented the experiences of the Stolen Generations, called for reparations, public apologies, and ongoing support for Indigenous communities affected by these policies.

Although Australia has not established a formal TRC, truth-telling initiatives such as the Uluru Statement from the Heart (2017) have emphasized the need for truth-telling as part of the broader reconciliation process. The statement calls for constitutional recognition of Indigenous Australians, the establishment of a First Nations Voice to Parliament, and the creation of a Makarrata Commission to oversee truth-telling and agreement-making between Indigenous peoples and the government.

5. Challenges and Criticisms of Truth and Reconciliation Commissions

While TRCs have played a vital role in promoting restorative justice and reconciliation, they are not without challenges and criticisms. Some of the most common concerns include the limitations of non-punitive approaches, the risk of symbolic reconciliation without structural change, and the ongoing struggle for justice and equality for Indigenous peoples.

5.1 Limitations of Non-Punitive Approaches

One criticism of TRCs is that they may prioritize reconciliation at the expense of justice, particularly when they grant amnesty or fail to prosecute perpetrators. In some cases, survivors and their families may feel that the absence of punitive measures undermines the severity of the harm they experienced and fails to deliver justice.

5.2 Risk of Symbolic Reconciliation

Another challenge is the risk of symbolic reconciliation—where truth-telling and acknowledgment occur without meaningful structural change. While TRCs can foster important dialogue and healing, they must be accompanied by concrete actions, such as reparations, legal reforms, and policies that address the root causes of inequality and discrimination.

Conclusion: TRCs as Instruments of Restorative Justice

Truth and Reconciliation Commissions represent a powerful application of restorative justice principles, offering a path toward healing and reconciliation in the aftermath of systemic harm. By prioritizing truth-telling, accountability, and reparative action, TRCs seek to restore relationships and promote long-term social harmony.

For Indigenous communities, TRCs provide an essential platform for addressing the legacy of colonialism, land dispossession, and cultural suppression. While challenges remain, TRCs offer a model for how societies can come to terms with historical injustices and work toward a future built on mutual respect, equity, and justice.

Restorative Justice in the Context of Reconciliation

6.2 The Role of Apologies and Restitution

In the broader framework of restorative justice and reconciliation, apologies and restitution serve as critical components for addressing historical injustices and healing the relationships between victims and perpetrators. These mechanisms are not merely symbolic gestures but can play a transformative role in the process of rebuilding trust, acknowledging harm, and promoting societal healing. For Indigenous peoples, who have endured centuries of colonization, cultural suppression, and systemic discrimination, the need for meaningful apologies and adequate restitution is vital in fostering reconciliation.

This section explores how apologies and restitution function within restorative justice frameworks, particularly in the context of Indigenous communities. We will examine the significance of public and governmental apologies, the challenges of ensuring that these apologies are meaningful, and the role of restitution in repairing harm and promoting long-term reconciliation.

1. The Power of Apologies in Restorative Justice

Apologies are a central aspect of restorative justice because they offer a formal acknowledgment of the harm caused and provide a foundation for healing and reconciliation. A well-delivered apology can validate the experiences of victims, demonstrate accountability, and signal a commitment to making amends. In the context of historical and systemic injustices, particularly those experienced by Indigenous peoples, apologies are often seen as a first step toward restoring trust and addressing the wrongs of the past.

1.1 The Elements of a Meaningful Apology

For an apology to be effective within a restorative justice framework, it must go beyond mere words and demonstrate a genuine commitment to addressing the harm. The following elements are essential for a meaningful apology:

- Acknowledgment of Harm: The apology must clearly and unequivocally acknowledge the specific harm caused. In the case of Indigenous peoples, this often includes acknowledging the impacts of colonization, forced assimilation, land dispossession, and cultural erasure.

- Taking Responsibility: A meaningful apology includes taking full responsibility for the harm. This involves recognizing the role of individuals, institutions, or governments in perpetuating injustice and accepting accountability for their actions or inaction.

- Expression of Regret and Empathy: An apology must express genuine remorse for the harm caused and demonstrate empathy toward the victims. This humanizes the relationship between the wrongdoer and the victim, fostering a sense of shared humanity and mutual understanding.

- Commitment to Change: A meaningful apology must be accompanied by a commitment to preventing future harm and taking concrete steps to address the root causes of the injustice. This may include policy reforms, educational initiatives, or systemic changes aimed at preventing the recurrence of the harm.

1.2 Governmental Apologies to Indigenous Peoples

Governmental apologies play a significant role in addressing systemic harm, especially when it comes to the historical injustices experienced by Indigenous communities.

These apologies are often delivered as part of broader reconciliation processes and can mark a turning point in the relationship between Indigenous peoples and the state.

A well-known example is the 2008 apology by Canadian Prime Minister Stephen Harper to survivors of the Indian Residential School System. In this apology, Harper acknowledged the physical, emotional, and cultural abuse suffered by Indigenous children who were forcibly removed from their families and placed in residential schools. The apology was a formal acknowledgment of the Canadian government's role in implementing these policies, which aimed to eradicate Indigenous cultures and assimilate Indigenous children into Euro-Canadian society.

Harper's apology was seen as an important step in the reconciliation process, providing validation to survivors and their families. However, for many, the apology alone was insufficient without meaningful actions to accompany it, such as compensation, legal reforms, and measures to support cultural revitalization.

Similarly, in 2008, Australian Prime Minister Kevin Rudd issued a national apology to the Stolen Generations, Aboriginal and Torres Strait Islander children who were forcibly removed from their families as part of government policies aimed at assimilation. Rudd's apology recognized the profound suffering caused by these policies and expressed deep sorrow for the harm inflicted on Indigenous communities.

While these apologies were critical in acknowledging the past and opening the door to reconciliation, they also highlighted the need for ongoing efforts to repair the damage done and ensure that Indigenous peoples have access to justice, resources, and opportunities for cultural and economic self-determination.

2. Restitution as a Path to Justice

While apologies are an important aspect of restorative justice, they are often viewed as insufficient without restitution—the act of providing tangible reparations to address the harm caused. Restitution can take many forms, including financial compensation, land restitution, educational and healthcare services, and legal reforms aimed at redressing systemic inequalities. In the context of reconciliation, restitution represents a concrete commitment to making amends and restoring the dignity of those who have been harmed.

2.1 Financial Compensation and Reparations

One of the most common forms of restitution is financial compensation, which is provided to individuals or communities as a way to address the economic harm they have suffered. In many cases, financial compensation is provided to survivors of human rights abuses, such as the victims of residential schools or other government policies that inflicted physical, emotional, or economic harm.

In Canada, as part of the Indian Residential Schools Settlement Agreement, survivors of residential schools were awarded financial compensation for the abuse and cultural loss they experienced. This restitution was seen as an essential step in addressing the legacy of the residential school system, although many survivors argued that financial compensation alone could not fully repair the damage done to their identities, families, and cultures.

While financial compensation is important, it must be accompanied by other forms of restitution that address the broader systemic harms experienced by Indigenous peoples. This includes the restitution of land, cultural rights, and access to essential services such as education, healthcare, and housing.

2.2 Land Restitution and Sovereignty

For Indigenous peoples, land is not only an economic resource but also a cultural and spiritual foundation. As such, land restitution is a crucial aspect of reconciliation and restorative justice. The dispossession of Indigenous lands has been one of the most significant harms inflicted by colonialism, and the return of land or compensation for lost lands is a key demand of many Indigenous movements worldwide.

In countries such as Canada, New Zealand, and Australia, land restitution has been a central part of efforts to address historical injustices. In New Zealand, for example, the Waitangi Tribunal was established to address Māori land claims under the Treaty of Waitangi. The tribunal has facilitated the return of significant tracts of land to Māori iwi (tribes) and provided financial compensation in cases where land could not be returned.

Similarly, in Canada, land claims settlements have been negotiated between the government and Indigenous nations as part of the reconciliation process. These settlements often involve the return of land, financial compensation, and the recognition of Indigenous sovereignty and self-governance.

Restitution of land is not only about economic justice but also about restoring the cultural and spiritual connection that Indigenous peoples have to their ancestral territories. By returning land to Indigenous communities, governments acknowledge the central role that land plays in Indigenous identity, culture, and well-being.

2.3 Cultural and Educational Restitution

Another important form of restitution is the support for cultural and educational revitalization. Colonization and assimilation policies have severely impacted Indigenous languages, cultural practices, and knowledge systems. Restitution in this area involves providing resources to Indigenous communities to revitalize their languages, cultures, and traditional knowledge.

In Canada, the Truth and Reconciliation Commission (TRC) called for the establishment of programs to revitalize Indigenous languages and promote Indigenous cultural education. This includes supporting Indigenous language immersion programs, funding for cultural preservation projects, and the integration of Indigenous knowledge into school curricula.

Similarly, in Australia, the Bringing Them Home report recommended the establishment of services to support the emotional and cultural well-being of the Stolen Generations and their descendants, including access to cultural programs and services aimed at reconnecting Indigenous children with their families, languages, and traditions.

Educational restitution is also a key aspect of reconciliation, as access to quality education has historically been denied to many Indigenous communities. Restitution in this area involves improving access to education, creating culturally relevant curricula, and supporting Indigenous students in pursuing higher education and career opportunities.

3. Challenges in Delivering Meaningful Apologies and Restitution

While apologies and restitution are essential components of restorative justice and reconciliation, they also present challenges, particularly when it comes to ensuring that they are delivered in a meaningful and lasting way.

3.1 The Risk of Hollow Apologies

One of the main challenges is the risk of hollow apologies—apologies that are delivered without any genuine commitment to change or reparative action. In some cases, governmental or institutional apologies may be seen as symbolic gestures intended to appease public sentiment rather than as sincere attempts to address historical wrongs.

To avoid this, apologies must be accompanied by concrete actions that demonstrate a commitment to reconciliation. This includes making the necessary policy changes, providing financial restitution, and addressing the systemic inequalities that continue to affect Indigenous communities.

3.2 Ensuring Adequate and Appropriate Restitution

Another challenge is ensuring that restitution is both adequate and appropriate for the harm caused. Financial compensation, while important, may not be sufficient to address the cultural, spiritual, and emotional harm inflicted on Indigenous communities. In some cases, restitution may need to focus on the return of land, the revitalization of cultural practices, or the recognition of Indigenous sovereignty.

It is also important that restitution is determined in consultation with Indigenous communities, ensuring that it reflects their needs, priorities, and cultural values. Restitution must be seen as part of an ongoing process of reconciliation, rather than a one-time payment or settlement that absolves governments of their responsibilities.

4. The Path Forward: Toward Genuine Apologies and Restorative Restitution

The role of apologies and restitution in restorative justice is central to the process of reconciliation, particularly for Indigenous peoples. For these mechanisms to be effective, they must go beyond mere words or financial payments; they must demonstrate a genuine commitment to healing, repairing harm, and addressing the root causes of systemic injustice.

As societies continue to confront the legacy of colonization and historical injustice, governments, institutions, and communities must work together to deliver meaningful apologies and provide appropriate restitution. This requires ongoing dialogue, a commitment to structural change, and the recognition of Indigenous rights, cultures, and sovereignty.

Conclusion: Apologies and Restitution as Catalysts for Reconciliation

Apologies and restitution are powerful tools for promoting reconciliation and restorative justice, particularly in the context of Indigenous communities. When delivered sincerely and accompanied by tangible actions, they can help rebuild trust, heal historical wounds, and foster a more just and equitable society.

For Indigenous peoples, who have endured generations of harm, the process of reconciliation must involve not only the acknowledgment of past wrongs but also the active restoration of their rights, cultures, and territories. By embracing the principles of restorative justice and committing to meaningful apologies and restitution, societies can take important steps toward healing and reconciliation for all.

Restorative Justice in the Context of Reconciliation

6.3 Moving Toward Reconciliation: National and Community-Based Efforts

The journey toward reconciliation is a complex and multifaceted process that involves efforts at both the national and community levels. For Indigenous peoples who have experienced generations of systemic harm through colonization, cultural suppression, and forced assimilation, reconciliation is not just a matter of apology or compensation; it is an ongoing process of rebuilding relationships, restoring trust, and addressing the deep-rooted inequalities that persist.

Restorative justice offers a framework for this process by emphasizing healing, accountability, and the restoration of relationships. Reconciliation efforts involve creating synergies between governmental initiatives and grassroots, community-based approaches, which work together to address the unique needs and challenges faced by Indigenous communities. In this chapter, we explore how national and community-based efforts contribute to the broader goal of reconciliation, highlighting successes, challenges, and the path forward.

1. National-Level Efforts Toward Reconciliation

At the national level, governments are increasingly recognizing the need to address historical injustices against Indigenous peoples through formal reconciliation processes. These efforts typically include truth and reconciliation commissions, official apologies, legislative reforms, and the implementation of policies aimed at improving the well-being of Indigenous communities. However, the success of these initiatives often depends on the extent to which they are accompanied by meaningful actions and systemic change.

1.1 Government Commitments to Reconciliation

National governments have a critical role in initiating reconciliation by acknowledging their historical role in perpetuating injustice and committing to the long-term process of healing. Over the past few decades, several countries have launched national-level efforts to promote reconciliation with Indigenous peoples, often beginning with truth-telling and public apologies.

- Canada's Commitment to Reconciliation: Canada's Truth and Reconciliation Commission (TRC) stands as one of the most significant national-level efforts to address the legacy of the Indian Residential School System. The TRC, which was established in 2008, gathered testimonies from survivors and made 94 Calls to Action aimed at addressing the ongoing impacts of colonization. These recommendations called for legal reforms, educational initiatives, cultural preservation programs, and support for Indigenous self-determination. The Canadian government has made commitments to implement these recommendations, including official apologies, policy changes, and efforts to revitalize Indigenous languages and cultures.

- New Zealand and the Treaty of Waitangi: In New Zealand, national reconciliation efforts are centered on the Treaty of Waitangi, signed between Māori chiefs and the British Crown in 1840. Over the years, the New Zealand government has taken steps to address breaches of the Treaty through the establishment of the Waitangi Tribunal, which investigates land claims and other grievances brought by Māori iwi (tribes). This process has led to the return of land, financial compensation, and formal apologies from the government. These efforts are part of a broader commitment to honor the Treaty and recognize Māori self-determination.

- Australia's Path Toward Reconciliation: In Australia, national reconciliation efforts have focused on addressing the injustices of the Stolen Generations, during which Aboriginal and Torres Strait Islander children were forcibly removed from their families. Prime Minister Kevin Rudd's 2008 apology was a landmark moment in recognizing the harm caused by government policies. However, the reconciliation process in Australia continues to evolve, with ongoing efforts to promote constitutional recognition of Indigenous Australians, address land rights, and improve social and economic outcomes for Indigenous communities.

1.2 Legal and Policy Reforms

Meaningful reconciliation at the national level often requires legal and policy reforms that address the systemic inequalities faced by Indigenous peoples. These reforms can include:

- Land Rights and Sovereignty: Restoring Indigenous land rights is central to the reconciliation process. Governments can enact legislation that recognizes Indigenous sovereignty, facilitates land restitution, and protects sacred sites. In some countries, Indigenous peoples have gained legal recognition of their land claims through comprehensive settlements or tribunal processes.

- Self-Determination: Reconciliation requires governments to support Indigenous self-determination by recognizing Indigenous governance structures, legal systems, and decision-making processes. This may involve reforms to the constitution, legal recognition of Indigenous legal traditions, or increased funding for Indigenous-led governance initiatives.

- Cultural Revitalization and Education: National reconciliation efforts often include initiatives aimed at revitalizing Indigenous cultures and languages. This can involve integrating Indigenous knowledge into public education systems, funding cultural preservation programs, and promoting Indigenous language education. Additionally, educational curricula that reflect the true history of Indigenous peoples and the impact of colonization are vital for fostering understanding and reconciliation.

- Economic and Social Equity: Addressing the social and economic disparities experienced by Indigenous peoples is essential for reconciliation. This includes improving access to healthcare, education, housing, and employment opportunities, as well as addressing the overrepresentation of Indigenous peoples in criminal justice systems. Policy changes that address these disparities contribute to long-term reconciliation by promoting equity and justice.

2. Community-Based Approaches to Reconciliation

While national-level efforts are essential for creating broad systemic change, true reconciliation must also take place at the community level, where relationships between Indigenous and non-Indigenous peoples are rebuilt through dialogue, collaboration, and mutual understanding.

Community-based initiatives are often led by Indigenous organizations, local governments, and grassroots movements, and they focus on addressing the unique needs and challenges of individual communities.

2.1 Grassroots Movements and Local Leadership

Grassroots movements play a crucial role in reconciliation efforts by advocating for Indigenous rights, raising awareness about historical injustices, and fostering cross-cultural dialogue. These movements are often driven by Indigenous leaders and activists who work to empower their communities and hold governments accountable for their commitments to reconciliation.

- Idle No More (Canada): One of the most prominent grassroots movements advocating for Indigenous rights and reconciliation is Idle No More, which originated in Canada in 2012. The movement began as a response to government legislation that threatened Indigenous land and water rights, but it has since evolved into a broader campaign for Indigenous sovereignty, environmental justice, and cultural preservation. Idle No More has mobilized Indigenous and non-Indigenous allies across the country, using peaceful protests, teach-ins, and public events to raise awareness about the need for reconciliation and systemic change.

- The Uluru Statement from the Heart (Australia): In Australia, the Uluru Statement from the Heart, issued by Indigenous leaders in 2017, calls for constitutional recognition of Indigenous Australians and the establishment of a First Nations Voice to Parliament. This grassroots initiative has garnered significant support from Indigenous and non-Indigenous communities alike, and it represents a powerful call for reconciliation through political reform, truth-telling, and structural change.

2.2 Community-Based Restorative Justice Initiatives

Restorative justice initiatives at the community level provide a practical framework for reconciliation by addressing conflicts, promoting healing, and restoring relationships between Indigenous and non-Indigenous peoples. These initiatives often take the form of peacemaking circles, healing circles, or Marae-based justice programs, and they are grounded in Indigenous cultural traditions.

- Peacemaking Circles: In Indigenous communities, peacemaking circles are often used to address disputes, resolve conflicts, and promote healing. These circles bring together victims, offenders, and community members to discuss the harm that has occurred and to develop a plan for reconciliation. Peacemaking circles emphasize accountability, empathy, and the restoration of relationships, and they are increasingly being used in both Indigenous and non-Indigenous communities to address a wide range of conflicts.

- Marae-Based Justice Programs (New Zealand): In New Zealand, Marae-based justice programs provide a community-based approach to addressing harm and promoting reconciliation. These programs take place on the Marae (a traditional Māori meeting ground) and involve the participation of elders, families, and community members. The focus is on healing, accountability, and restoring the mana (dignity and respect) of all parties involved. These programs reflect the values of Māori restorative justice and offer a culturally grounded alternative to formal court proceedings.

- Healing and Reconciliation Circles (Canada): In Canada, healing and reconciliation circles have been used to address the legacy of residential schools and other forms of systemic harm. These circles provide a safe space for survivors to share their experiences, seek healing, and engage in dialogue with members of the broader community. By fostering mutual understanding and empathy, healing circles contribute to the larger process of reconciliation.

2.3 Cross-Cultural Education and Collaboration

Cross-cultural education and collaboration are critical for fostering reconciliation at the community level. These initiatives aim to bridge the gap between Indigenous and non-Indigenous peoples by promoting mutual understanding, respect, and collaboration. They often involve partnerships between schools, community organizations, and local governments.

- Cultural Exchange Programs: Cross-cultural exchange programs that bring together Indigenous and non-Indigenous students, leaders, and community members can promote reconciliation by fostering dialogue and understanding. These programs may involve cultural immersion experiences, language learning, and shared community projects that allow participants to learn from one another and build relationships based on respect.

- Reconciliation through Education: Educational initiatives that center Indigenous histories, cultures, and perspectives are crucial for promoting reconciliation at the community level. Many schools and universities are integrating Indigenous knowledge into their curricula, offering courses on Indigenous history, languages, and worldviews. These initiatives help to challenge stereotypes, promote cultural awareness, and build a foundation for reconciliation.

3. Challenges and Opportunities in Reconciliation Efforts

While there have been significant strides in reconciliation at both the national and community levels, challenges remain. These include ensuring that reconciliation efforts are inclusive, addressing ongoing systemic inequalities, and overcoming resistance to change.

3.1 Ensuring Inclusivity in Reconciliation Efforts

One of the key challenges in reconciliation is ensuring that all voices, particularly those of marginalized or isolated communities, are

included in the process. Indigenous communities are diverse, and their experiences of colonization and injustice vary widely. Reconciliation efforts must take into account this diversity and ensure that all Indigenous peoples, including women, youth, and LGBTQ+ individuals, are actively involved in shaping the future.

3.2 Addressing Ongoing Inequalities

Reconciliation efforts must also address the ongoing social, economic, and political inequalities faced by Indigenous peoples. While truth-telling, apologies, and symbolic gestures are important, they must be accompanied by meaningful actions that address poverty, health disparities, land rights, and access to resources. Structural change is essential for achieving lasting reconciliation.

3.3 Overcoming Resistance and Building Consensus

Reconciliation efforts often face resistance from both Indigenous and non-Indigenous communities. Some non-Indigenous individuals may resist reconciliation efforts due to a lack of understanding or fear of losing political or economic power. On the other hand, some Indigenous peoples may be skeptical of reconciliation initiatives that do not go far enough in addressing systemic harm or that are perceived as superficial. Building consensus and fostering trust between these groups is essential for moving reconciliation forward.

Conclusion: Building a Future of Reconciliation

Reconciliation is not a destination but an ongoing process that requires the combined efforts of national governments, Indigenous leaders, grassroots movements, and local communities. By integrating national-level commitments with community-based initiatives, it is possible to create a holistic and inclusive approach to reconciliation that addresses both historical injustices and present-day inequalities.

Moving forward, the path to reconciliation will involve continued dialogue, collaboration, and a commitment to justice, equity, and mutual respect. Through national and community-based efforts, societies can work together to heal the wounds of the past and build a future grounded in understanding, shared humanity, and reconciliation.

CHAPTER 07

CHALLENGES AND FUTURE DIRECTIONS

7.1 Systemic Barriers and Legal Constraints

While restorative justice, particularly in the context of reconciliation with Indigenous communities, offers powerful tools for healing and social change, the implementation of these practices faces several systemic barriers and legal constraints. These challenges complicate efforts to incorporate restorative principles into modern legal systems, create meaningful reparations, and promote long-term societal healing.

The transition from punitive justice models to those grounded in restorative justice, especially as applied to

Indigenous communities, requires not only a shift in policy but a transformation of the underlying social, legal, and economic structures that have historically marginalized these communities. In this chapter, we examine the key systemic barriers and legal constraints that hinder the implementation of restorative justice, with a focus on those affecting Indigenous peoples. We also explore potential strategies for overcoming these obstacles as we look toward the future of restorative justice and reconciliation.

1. Systemic Barriers to Restorative Justice

Systemic barriers refer to the structural and institutional obstacles that prevent the effective implementation of restorative justice practices. These barriers often stem from deeply ingrained social, economic, and political inequities that have historically disadvantaged Indigenous peoples and other marginalized groups. Addressing these barriers is crucial to creating a justice system that is truly restorative and inclusive.

1.1 Colonial Legacies and Historical Injustices

One of the most significant systemic barriers to restorative justice is the enduring legacy of colonialism. Colonization systematically dispossessed Indigenous peoples of their lands, cultures, and governance systems, replacing

Indigenous legal traditions with Western legal frameworks that were often punitive and retributive in nature. This history of colonization continues to shape the relationship between Indigenous peoples and state institutions, including the legal system.

Colonial legacies have left Indigenous communities with lasting socio-economic disadvantages, including high rates of poverty, poor access to education and healthcare, and overrepresentation in the criminal justice system. These disparities make it difficult to implement restorative justice practices that require community involvement, resources, and sustained engagement. Furthermore, the ongoing impact of historical trauma, including intergenerational trauma resulting from policies like forced assimilation and residential schools, complicates efforts to promote reconciliation and healing.

Overcoming this barrier requires a comprehensive approach that addresses both the historical injustices of colonization and their contemporary effects. Restorative justice cannot succeed without first acknowledging and addressing the root causes of Indigenous marginalization, including land dispossession, cultural suppression, and systemic racism.

1.2 Socio-Economic Inequality

Closely tied to colonial legacies, socio-economic inequality poses a significant barrier to the implementation of restorative justice. Indigenous peoples, particularly in countries like Canada, Australia, and the United States, continue to experience high levels of poverty, unemployment, and limited access to basic services such as healthcare and education. These socio-economic disparities hinder the capacity of Indigenous communities to participate fully in restorative justice initiatives.

Restorative justice relies on community participation, dialogue, and long-term engagement, all of which require resources, infrastructure, and social support. In communities where poverty and social inequality are prevalent, there may be limited access to the resources needed to facilitate these processes, such as mediators, legal aid, or mental health services. This creates a vicious cycle, where marginalized communities are unable to access restorative justice, and the lack of restorative justice perpetuates social and economic marginalization.

Addressing this barrier requires governments and institutions to invest in the social and economic empowerment of Indigenous communities. This includes funding community-based restorative justice programs, providing access to education and job training, and ensuring that Indigenous peoples have the resources they need to engage in healing and reconciliation processes.

1.3 Cultural Disconnection and Erosion of Traditional Legal Systems

The disconnection from traditional cultures and legal systems is another significant barrier to implementing restorative justice in Indigenous communities. Colonization often disrupted the transmission of Indigenous knowledge, languages, and legal traditions, eroding the cultural foundations that once supported community-based justice systems. As a result, many Indigenous communities have struggled to maintain or revitalize their traditional forms of conflict resolution, which are integral to restorative justice practices.

In some cases, Indigenous legal traditions have been marginalized or even criminalized by colonial governments. For example, traditional practices such as circle sentencing or peacemaking may not be recognized as legitimate forms of justice within the formal legal system, limiting their use in addressing disputes or criminal offenses.

Revitalizing Indigenous legal traditions is essential to overcoming this barrier. This requires efforts to restore cultural knowledge, support Indigenous language revitalization, and empower Indigenous leaders and elders to take an active role in justice processes. Governments and legal systems must also recognize and respect the legitimacy of Indigenous legal systems, allowing them to coexist alongside state-run legal institutions.

1.4 Public Perception and Resistance to Restorative Justice

Public perception of restorative justice, particularly among non-Indigenous populations, can also pose a barrier to its implementation. In many societies, there is a widespread belief that justice should be retributive—focusing on punishment and deterrence—rather than restorative. This belief is often fueled by media portrayals of crime, which emphasize punishment as a means of protecting public safety.

In this context, restorative justice is sometimes seen as "soft on crime" or as insufficiently punitive, particularly when applied to serious offenses. These perceptions can lead to resistance from both the public and the legal establishment, who may question the legitimacy of restorative justice processes and their ability to hold offenders accountable.

Overcoming this barrier requires a concerted effort to educate the public about the principles and benefits of restorative justice. This includes promoting greater awareness of the ways in which restorative justice can promote healing, reduce recidivism, and strengthen communities. Additionally, governments and legal institutions must take steps to demonstrate the effectiveness of restorative justice through pilot programs, case studies, and data collection that highlight its success in reducing harm and promoting long-term peace.

2. Legal Constraints in the Implementation of Restorative Justice

In addition to systemic barriers, there are legal constraints that limit the application of restorative justice within formal legal systems. These constraints are often rooted in the structure and priorities of modern legal institutions, which tend to prioritize retribution, legal formalism, and individual rights over collective healing and reconciliation.

2.1 Punitive Nature of Modern Legal Systems

Most contemporary legal systems, particularly in Western countries, are based on a punitive model of justice. This model emphasizes punishment and deterrence as the primary means of addressing crime, focusing on retribution for wrongdoing rather than on repairing the harm caused by the offense. As a result, restorative justice—which prioritizes dialogue, accountability, and the restoration of relationships—can struggle to find a place within these systems.

Punitive justice systems often rely on formal legal procedures, strict rules of evidence, and prescribed sentences, leaving little room for alternative approaches like restorative justice. In cases involving serious crimes, such as violence or sexual assault, courts may be hesitant to allow restorative justice processes, viewing them as too lenient or insufficiently protective of victims' rights.

To overcome this constraint, legal systems need to adopt more flexible sentencing frameworks that allow for the use of restorative justice in appropriate cases. This may involve creating hybrid models of justice that incorporate both punitive and restorative elements, allowing for a more balanced approach to addressing harm. Additionally, legal reforms should ensure that restorative justice is available as an option at various stages of the justice process, from pre-trial diversion to post-sentencing reintegration.

2.2 Lack of Legal Recognition for Indigenous Restorative Justice Practices

Another key legal constraint is the lack of formal recognition for Indigenous restorative justice practices within state-run legal systems. Many Indigenous legal traditions, including peacemaking, circle sentencing, and community healing practices, are not recognized as legitimate forms of justice within Western legal frameworks. This lack of recognition limits the ability of Indigenous communities to use these practices in resolving disputes or addressing criminal offenses.

In some cases, Indigenous restorative justice practices are only allowed as part of alternative sentencing programs or diversion schemes, where offenders have already been processed through the formal legal system. This limits the autonomy of Indigenous communities to administer justice according to their own values and traditions.

Addressing this constraint requires legal reforms that formally recognize Indigenous justice systems and allow them to operate alongside state-run legal institutions. Governments must work in partnership with Indigenous leaders to develop frameworks that respect Indigenous sovereignty, support self-determination, and ensure that Indigenous justice practices are given equal weight in the resolution of disputes.

2.3 Balancing Restorative and Retributive Approaches

A persistent challenge in integrating restorative justice into formal legal systems is the need to balance restorative and retributive approaches to justice. While restorative justice focuses on healing, accountability, and reconciliation, retributive justice prioritizes punishment and deterrence. Finding the right balance between these two approaches is critical for ensuring that both the needs of victims and the demands of public safety are met.

In some cases, restorative justice may be viewed as more appropriate for addressing minor offenses, while retributive justice is seen as necessary for dealing with serious crimes. However, this

Challenges and Future Directions

7.2 Sustainability of Indigenous Restorative Justice Systems

The sustainability of Indigenous restorative justice systems is essential to ensuring the long-term success of these practices in promoting healing, reconciliation, and justice within Indigenous communities and broader society. Indigenous restorative justice systems, which are deeply rooted in cultural traditions and community-centered approaches, offer a meaningful alternative to punitive legal frameworks. However, their sustainability faces a number of challenges, including the need for ongoing community capacity building, the support of legal and political institutions, and the preservation of cultural integrity in an evolving world.

This section examines the factors necessary to sustain Indigenous restorative justice systems over the long term. We will explore the importance of community engagement, cultural revitalization, institutional support, and the need for adaptability to ensure that these systems remain effective in addressing the needs of Indigenous peoples.

1. Community Engagement and Capacity Building

One of the most critical factors in the sustainability of Indigenous restorative justice systems is community engagement. These systems rely heavily on the active participation of community members, including elders, spiritual leaders, families, and other stakeholders, in resolving conflicts, promoting healing, and ensuring accountability. The strength of Indigenous restorative justice lies in its collective nature, where responsibility for justice is shared by the entire community.

1.1 Active Participation of Elders and Leaders

Elders and community leaders play a central role in Indigenous restorative justice systems. They are often tasked with facilitating peacemaking circles, healing circles, or community-based justice programs, drawing on their knowledge of cultural traditions, spiritual practices, and community values. The involvement of elders is vital to maintaining the cultural integrity of restorative justice processes, as they provide wisdom, guidance, and authority that is respected by the community.

To ensure the sustainability of these systems, it is essential that elders and community leaders are supported through capacity-building initiatives. This can include training programs that strengthen their facilitation skills, provide them with resources for conflict resolution, and help them navigate the interaction between Indigenous and state-run legal systems. Additionally, efforts to empower a new generation of Indigenous leaders are crucial for ensuring that these practices continue to thrive in the future.

1.2 Intergenerational Engagement

Sustaining Indigenous restorative justice systems also requires the engagement of younger generations. The intergenerational transmission of cultural knowledge and values is key to the longevity of these systems, as younger community members must be involved in the justice process and educated about the importance of restorative principles. Programs that involve youth in peacemaking or conflict resolution can foster a sense of responsibility and leadership, ensuring that restorative justice practices are passed down to future generations.

2. Cultural Revitalization and Preservation

The sustainability of Indigenous restorative justice systems is closely tied to the broader efforts of cultural revitalization and preservation. Colonization, forced assimilation, and the suppression of Indigenous cultures have eroded the foundations of many Indigenous legal traditions, making it difficult for some communities to sustain their traditional justice practices. Revitalizing and preserving Indigenous cultures is therefore essential to sustaining restorative justice systems.

2.1 Language Revitalization

Language is a key component of cultural identity and is deeply intertwined with Indigenous justice practices. Many Indigenous restorative justice systems rely on the use of traditional languages in ceremonies, conflict resolution processes, and community dialogues. For example, terms like whakapapa (genealogy) or mana (dignity) in Māori culture are fundamental to understanding the values that underpin justice and social harmony.

Language revitalization efforts are therefore critical for the sustainability of Indigenous restorative justice systems.

Programs that promote Indigenous language education, immersion schools, and language preservation projects can help ensure that the cultural knowledge embedded in these languages is passed on to future generations.

2.2 Preserving Cultural Traditions in Justice

Indigenous restorative justice practices are often grounded in specific cultural and spiritual traditions, including ceremonies, storytelling, and community rituals. These traditions provide the framework for addressing harm, promoting healing, and restoring balance within the community. However, many of these traditions have been weakened or lost due to colonization, residential schools, and the disruption of Indigenous social structures.

To sustain Indigenous restorative justice systems, it is essential to support efforts to preserve and revitalize these cultural traditions. This includes ensuring that Indigenous communities have the resources and autonomy to maintain their ceremonies, spiritual practices, and traditional governance structures. Governments and institutions must respect and protect these traditions, providing Indigenous peoples with the space and support to practice justice in ways that are consistent with their cultural values.

3. Institutional and Legal Support

While Indigenous restorative justice systems are deeply rooted in cultural and community practices, their long-term sustainability also depends on the support of state institutions and legal frameworks. In many countries, Indigenous justice practices operate alongside, or within, formal legal systems. Ensuring that these practices are recognized and supported by the state is crucial for their sustainability.

3.1 Legal Recognition and Integration

One of the key factors in sustaining Indigenous restorative justice systems is the legal recognition of Indigenous justice practices within national legal frameworks. Many Indigenous justice systems are not formally recognized by the state, limiting their ability to address conflicts or administer justice in a way that is consistent with their cultural traditions. Without formal recognition, Indigenous justice systems may be marginalized or excluded from important decision-making processes.

Legal reforms that formally recognize Indigenous justice systems, such as the recognition of circle sentencing, peacemaking courts, or other community-based justice programs, are essential for their sustainability. Governments must work collaboratively with Indigenous leaders to develop policies that allow Indigenous legal traditions to operate independently or in partnership with state-run legal systems.

3.2 Resource Allocation and Funding

The sustainability of Indigenous restorative justice systems also depends on the availability of resources. These systems require funding for facilitators, training programs, legal aid, and the development of community-based justice initiatives. In many cases, Indigenous communities face significant economic challenges that limit their capacity to implement restorative justice programs without external support.

Governments and non-governmental organizations can play a key role in supporting the sustainability of Indigenous justice systems by providing funding and resources for community-based justice programs. This may include grants for Indigenous-led initiatives, financial support for legal education, and resources for cultural preservation projects. Sustainable funding models are necessary to ensure that Indigenous restorative justice systems can continue to operate effectively in the long term.

4. Adaptability to Changing Social Contexts

For Indigenous restorative justice systems to remain sustainable, they must be able to adapt to changing social, political, and legal contexts. As Indigenous communities face new challenges—such as globalization, environmental degradation, and shifting social norms—restorative justice systems must evolve to address these issues while remaining true to their cultural foundations.

4.1 Adapting to Contemporary Issues

Indigenous restorative justice systems must be able to address contemporary challenges that may not have existed in traditional justice frameworks. For example, issues such as cyberbullying, environmental conflicts, or drug-related offenses may require new approaches within the restorative justice process. Adapting to these modern challenges while maintaining the core principles of healing, accountability, and community involvement is essential for sustainability.

4.2 Balancing Tradition and Innovation

Sustaining Indigenous restorative justice systems requires a balance between preserving traditional practices and embracing innovation. While it is important to maintain the cultural integrity of Indigenous justice traditions, these systems must also be open to new ideas and methods that can enhance their effectiveness in a rapidly changing world. This may include incorporating restorative justice technologies, developing new approaches to conflict resolution, or collaborating with non-Indigenous justice systems in ways that promote mutual learning and respect.

5. Political Will and Advocacy

Finally, the sustainability of Indigenous restorative justice systems depends on political will and the advocacy of Indigenous leaders and their allies. Governments must demonstrate a genuine commitment to reconciliation and the empowerment of Indigenous peoples by supporting Indigenous justice systems and addressing the systemic barriers that undermine their effectiveness.

5.1 Indigenous Advocacy for Justice

Indigenous leaders and activists play a crucial role in advocating for the recognition and sustainability of Indigenous restorative justice systems. Through political engagement, grassroots movements, and legal challenges, Indigenous advocates work to ensure that their communities have the autonomy and resources to administer justice in culturally relevant ways.

5.2 Government Commitment to Reconciliation

Governments must also be held accountable for their commitments to reconciliation and the support of Indigenous justice systems. This requires not only legal reforms and funding but also a shift in attitudes toward Indigenous sovereignty and self-determination. Governments must recognize the importance of Indigenous justice as a fundamental aspect of nation-building and reconciliation.

Conclusion: Building a Sustainable Future for Indigenous Restorative Justice

The sustainability of Indigenous restorative justice systems is essential for promoting long-term healing, reconciliation, and justice within Indigenous communities and beyond. To achieve this, it is necessary to address systemic barriers, provide legal recognition, invest in community capacity building, and ensure that Indigenous cultures and traditions are preserved and revitalized.

As we look to the future, it is clear that Indigenous restorative justice systems have the potential to offer a more compassionate, community-centered approach to justice. By supporting these systems and ensuring their sustainability, societies can move toward a more just and equitable future that respects the rights, cultures, and sovereignty of Indigenous peoples.

Challenges and Future Directions

7.3 The Future of Restorative Justice in Indigenous Communities

As Indigenous communities around the world continue to revitalize their cultural practices and reclaim their rights to justice and self-determination, the future of restorative justice holds immense promise. Restorative justice, grounded in Indigenous values of healing, reconciliation, and collective responsibility, offers a path toward addressing the deep-rooted harms of colonization and systemic oppression. However, realizing this vision requires overcoming current challenges and laying the foundation for sustained, culturally responsive, and community-centered justice systems that honor Indigenous traditions.

This section explores the future directions of restorative justice in Indigenous communities, focusing on the potential for growth, the necessary structural and institutional changes, and the opportunities for greater collaboration between Indigenous and state-run legal systems. We will also examine how Indigenous restorative justice can contribute to broader movements for social justice and equity, ultimately offering transformative models for justice worldwide.

1. Expanding the Role of Indigenous Restorative Justice

As restorative justice practices gain recognition globally, Indigenous communities are well-positioned to expand their role in shaping justice systems that are inclusive, community-centered, and culturally grounded. The future of Indigenous restorative justice involves not only preserving and revitalizing traditional practices but also integrating these practices into modern legal frameworks in ways that benefit both Indigenous and non-Indigenous peoples.

1.1 Revitalization of Traditional Practices

The revitalization of traditional restorative justice practices will be central to the future of justice in Indigenous communities. For centuries, colonization and forced assimilation disrupted Indigenous governance and justice systems, leading to the erosion of cultural practices related to conflict resolution, healing, and social harmony. The future of restorative justice depends on the continued restoration of these practices, grounded in Indigenous languages, spiritual beliefs, and cultural traditions.

To ensure this revitalization, Indigenous communities must continue to invest in cultural education and the transmission of traditional knowledge to younger generations. This includes the re-establishment of elders' councils, peacemaking circles, and other community-based justice mechanisms that have long been central to Indigenous approaches to justice. The use of Indigenous languages and spiritual rituals in these processes reinforces the cultural integrity of restorative justice, ensuring that it remains deeply connected to Indigenous ways of life.

1.2 Integration with Modern Legal Systems

While preserving traditional practices is essential, the future of Indigenous restorative justice will also involve greater integration with modern legal systems. Across many countries, Indigenous justice systems are beginning to interact with state-run legal frameworks, creating opportunities for collaboration and mutual learning.

For example, hybrid justice models that combine elements of state law with Indigenous restorative practices are already being used in some regions. In Canada, programs like Gladue courts incorporate Indigenous perspectives into sentencing decisions for Indigenous offenders, while in New Zealand, Marae-based justice programs offer an alternative to conventional criminal courts for Māori communities. Expanding these hybrid models allows for greater flexibility in addressing complex cases and ensuring that justice is both culturally responsive and effective in modern contexts.

The integration of Indigenous justice into formal legal systems can also help address issues like over-incarceration, reduce recidivism, and provide a more holistic approach to justice that emphasizes rehabilitation and reintegration over punishment. As these models evolve, it will be important to ensure that Indigenous communities retain control over their justice processes, preventing cultural dilution or appropriation.

2. Structural and Institutional Changes for Long-Term Sustainability

To support the future of restorative justice in Indigenous communities, structural and institutional changes are needed at both the national and international levels. These changes must address the systemic barriers that Indigenous peoples face in accessing justice, ensuring that Indigenous justice systems are recognized, supported, and sustainable in the long term.

2.1 Legal Recognition of Indigenous Justice Systems

One of the most important steps for the future of Indigenous restorative justice is the legal recognition of Indigenous justice systems. In many countries, Indigenous communities have long fought for the right to govern their own affairs, including the administration of justice. Legal recognition allows Indigenous justice systems to operate with autonomy and authority, ensuring that they are not merely alternatives to state law but are fully respected as legitimate systems of justice.

This recognition must be accompanied by constitutional or legislative reforms that guarantee Indigenous peoples' rights to self-determination and the preservation of their legal traditions. In some countries, such as New Zealand and Canada, legal frameworks that acknowledge the role of Indigenous justice systems already exist, but more work is needed to expand and strengthen these frameworks. In other regions, governments will need to engage in meaningful dialogue with Indigenous leaders to develop new policies that support the full integration of Indigenous justice into national legal systems.

2.2 Institutional Support and Capacity Building

Sustaining Indigenous restorative justice systems over the long term requires investment in institutional support and capacity building. Governments and non-governmental organizations must provide resources to help Indigenous communities develop and maintain their justice programs. This includes funding for training mediators, establishing community-based justice centers, and supporting the involvement of elders and traditional leaders in the justice process.

Capacity building is also needed to ensure that Indigenous communities have the tools to engage effectively with state-run legal systems when necessary. This might involve providing legal education, developing cross-cultural training for lawyers and judges, and creating mechanisms for collaboration between Indigenous and non-Indigenous justice systems.

Ensuring that Indigenous justice systems have access to sustainable funding is critical. Many Indigenous communities face economic challenges, and without adequate financial resources, it may be difficult to sustain restorative justice programs. Governments must commit to providing long-term funding and institutional support to ensure that these systems can continue to operate effectively.

3. Building Collaborative Partnerships Between Indigenous and State-Run Justice Systems

The future of restorative justice in Indigenous communities will depend in part on the development of collaborative partnerships between Indigenous and state-run justice systems. These partnerships can create synergies that benefit both Indigenous and non-Indigenous communities by fostering mutual learning, sharing resources, and developing new approaches to justice that are more inclusive and restorative.

3.1 Collaborative Justice Programs

Collaborative justice programs offer a model for how Indigenous and state-run legal systems can work together to address complex social issues. These programs might involve joint initiatives to reduce crime, address poverty, or promote community health, with Indigenous justice systems playing a central role in shaping the solutions. For example, state-run courts could refer cases to Indigenous peacemaking or healing circles, allowing for culturally appropriate conflict resolution that emphasizes healing and reconciliation.

Collaborative programs can also serve as pilot projects for broader legal reforms. By demonstrating the effectiveness of restorative justice in reducing recidivism, promoting community engagement, and addressing the root causes of crime, these programs can help build the case for expanding restorative justice models within national legal systems.

3.2 Mutual Learning and Respect

For collaborative partnerships to be successful, they must be built on a foundation of mutual learning and respect.

State-run legal systems have much to learn from Indigenous approaches to justice, particularly in terms of community-centered practices, collective responsibility, and holistic healing. At the same time, Indigenous communities can benefit from access to resources, legal education, and institutional support offered by state-run systems.

These partnerships should be based on a recognition of equal standing between Indigenous and non-Indigenous justice systems. Rather than treating Indigenous justice as a subsidiary or alternative to state law, governments and legal institutions must respect the autonomy and authority of Indigenous justice systems. This requires ongoing dialogue, trust-building, and a commitment to respecting the rights of Indigenous peoples.

4. Indigenous Restorative Justice as a Model for Broader Social Justice Movements

As the world grapples with issues of inequality, systemic racism, and mass incarceration, Indigenous restorative justice offers a powerful model for broader social justice movements. The principles of healing, reconciliation, and community accountability that underpin Indigenous justice systems have relevance far beyond Indigenous communities and can serve as a foundation for reimagining justice systems worldwide.

4.1 Addressing Mass Incarceration and Racial Inequality

One of the most significant contributions of Indigenous restorative justice is its potential to address the over-incarceration of marginalized populations, particularly Indigenous peoples, people of color, and other minority groups. In many countries, punitive justice systems have disproportionately targeted these populations, leading to high rates of imprisonment, systemic racism, and social inequality.

Restorative justice offers an alternative approach that focuses on addressing the root causes of crime—such as poverty, trauma, and social exclusion—rather than simply punishing offenders. By promoting rehabilitation, reintegration, and community healing, Indigenous restorative justice can contribute to efforts to reduce mass incarceration and create more equitable justice systems.

4.2 Promoting Global Restorative Justice Practices

Indigenous restorative justice also has the potential to inspire global movements for restorative justice. As countries around the world seek alternatives to punitive justice models, they can look to Indigenous communities for guidance on how to build justice systems that are more compassionate, community-centered, and effective in promoting long-term peace and reconciliation.

In this way, Indigenous restorative justice can serve as a model for global efforts to transform justice systems and address the social and economic inequalities that contribute to conflict and crime. By drawing on the wisdom of Indigenous legal traditions, societies can move toward a future of justice that prioritizes healing, collective responsibility, and mutual respect.

Conclusion: A Vision for the Future of Indigenous Restorative Justice

The future of restorative justice in Indigenous communities holds great potential for creating a more just, equitable, and compassionate world. By revitalizing traditional practices, integrating with modern legal systems, and building collaborative partnerships, Indigenous communities can ensure that their restorative justice systems remain sustainable and effective for generations to come.

As Indigenous restorative justice systems continue to evolve, they will play a critical role in promoting reconciliation, healing historical wounds, and addressing the systemic barriers that have long marginalized Indigenous peoples. At the same time, these systems offer valuable lessons for broader social justice movements, demonstrating the power of justice that is rooted in community, healing, and respect for human dignity.

The future of Indigenous restorative justice is not only about addressing past harms but about building a future where justice is a tool for empowerment, healing, and transformation—both within Indigenous communities and across the world.

CHAPTER 08

CONCLUSION

Revisiting Restorative Justice: Bridging Tradition and Modernity

The journey toward understanding and implementing restorative justice within Indigenous communities reveals a powerful convergence between ancient traditions and modern needs for justice, healing, and reconciliation. Indigenous restorative justice practices, deeply rooted in cultural traditions, offer an alternative to Western punitive justice systems by focusing on healing, the restoration of relationships, and the well-being of both the victim and the offender, as well as the broader community. As societies worldwide continue to confront the failures of retributive justice systems—particularly their inability to address the root causes of crime, reduce recidivism, or promote long-term healing—there is a growing recognition of the importance of these Indigenous approaches.

In this conclusion, we reflect on the broader significance of Indigenous restorative justice and how its principles can serve as a bridge between tradition and modernity, offering solutions to contemporary issues in justice while honoring the cultural legacies that have guided Indigenous communities for generations.

1. Restorative Justice as a Bridge Between Past and Present

Restorative justice is not a new concept; it has been practiced for centuries by Indigenous communities as part of their holistic approach to justice, governance, and social harmony. These practices have long emphasized the importance of healing, reconciliation, and collective responsibility, offering a stark contrast to the punitive models of justice imposed during colonization. The resurgence of these practices today represents not only a return to traditional values but also a response to the limitations of modern justice systems.

As Indigenous communities around the world continue to recover from the legacies of colonization, the revitalization of restorative justice offers a way to reconnect with cultural traditions while addressing contemporary social challenges. These practices can be adapted to modern contexts, addressing new forms of conflict and harm, while remaining grounded in the values of community, balance, and respect. By embracing both the wisdom of the past and the realities of the present, Indigenous restorative justice systems provide a bridge between tradition and modernity, offering a path toward justice that is both culturally resonant and socially relevant.

2. The Evolving Role of Indigenous Restorative Justice

The future of restorative justice in Indigenous communities lies in its ability to evolve and adapt without losing its cultural core. As we have seen, the sustainability of these systems depends on community engagement, cultural revitalization, legal recognition, and institutional support. Indigenous communities must continue to lead the way in shaping their justice systems, ensuring that they remain responsive to the changing needs of their people while staying true to their cultural foundations.

The growing integration of Indigenous restorative justice into state-run legal systems also holds great potential for creating more inclusive and effective justice models. Collaborative partnerships between Indigenous and non-Indigenous justice systems can lead to innovative solutions that benefit all members of society, while also respecting the autonomy and authority of Indigenous communities. These partnerships should be built on mutual respect, recognizing the value of Indigenous legal traditions and their ability to address complex social issues in ways that punitive systems often cannot.

3. Restorative Justice and Reconciliation

At its core, restorative justice is about reconciliation—reconciliation between individuals, within communities, and between Indigenous peoples and the state. For Indigenous communities, restorative justice offers a means of addressing the historical injustices of colonization and working toward healing and empowerment. It is not just a method of conflict resolution but a broader framework for addressing the systemic harm inflicted on Indigenous peoples through land dispossession, cultural suppression, and forced assimilation.

Restorative justice practices such as truth-telling, apologies, and restitution provide concrete mechanisms for acknowledging harm and working toward reconciliation. These practices have the potential to restore trust between Indigenous and non-Indigenous communities, promote social cohesion, and lay the groundwork for long-term peace. However, reconciliation is an ongoing process that requires sustained commitment from both Indigenous communities and state institutions. It is not enough to make symbolic gestures or short-term interventions; true reconciliation demands structural change, legal reform, and a collective dedication to justice, equity, and healing.

4. The Global Relevance of Indigenous Restorative Justice

Indigenous restorative justice practices offer valuable lessons not only for Indigenous communities but also for global justice systems. As societies around the world grapple with issues like mass incarceration, racial inequality, and social unrest, the principles of restorative justice provide an alternative framework for addressing harm and promoting justice. By focusing on healing rather than punishment, and by involving the entire community in the justice process, Indigenous restorative justice systems demonstrate the potential for more compassionate, inclusive, and effective approaches to conflict resolution.

The global relevance of these practices lies in their emphasis on restoring relationships and addressing the root causes of harm, rather than merely responding to symptoms of crime. As modern justice systems face increasing criticism for their inability to promote rehabilitation or reduce recidivism, Indigenous restorative justice provides a model for reimagining justice in ways that prioritize human dignity, social harmony, and long-term peace.

5. Moving Forward: A Vision for Justice

As we look to the future, it is clear that Indigenous restorative justice has a vital role to play in shaping a more just and equitable world. The principles that have guided Indigenous communities for centuries—healing, reconciliation, collective responsibility—offer a transformative vision for justice that transcends the limitations of punitive legal frameworks. By embracing these principles, societies can move toward a justice system that is not only more effective but also more humane.

The future of restorative justice requires ongoing collaboration between Indigenous and non-Indigenous communities, legal reforms that support the autonomy of Indigenous justice systems, and a commitment to preserving cultural traditions while adapting to modern challenges. Through this process, Indigenous communities can continue to lead the way in developing justice systems that promote healing, restore relationships, and build stronger, more resilient societies.

Conclusion: Bridging Tradition and Modernity

In revisiting restorative justice, we see the potential for bridging the wisdom of Indigenous traditions with the challenges and opportunities of modern justice systems. Indigenous restorative justice offers a pathway toward healing the wounds of the past, addressing the injustices of the present, and building a more just and harmonious future. By honoring the cultural foundations of these practices while embracing innovation and collaboration, we can ensure that restorative justice remains a vital force for reconciliation, empowerment, and transformation in Indigenous communities and beyond.

Ultimately, the future of restorative justice is about creating systems that reflect our shared humanity, respect for diversity, and commitment to justice. In this vision, Indigenous and non-Indigenous communities alike can come together to build a world where justice is not only a tool for punishment but a means of healing, restoration, and peace.

CHAPTER 09

REFERENCES

1. Alfred, T. (2009). Peace, Power, Righteousness: An Indigenous Manifesto. Oxford University Press.

2. Battiste, M. (2013). Decolonizing Education: Nourishing the Learning Spirit. UBC Press.

3. Borrows, J. (2002). Recovering Canada: The Resurgence of Indigenous Law. University of Toronto Press.

4. Chartrand, L. N., Horn, K., & Daniels, J. (2012). Métis History and Experience and Residential Schools in Canada. Aboriginal Healing Foundation.

5. Coulthard, G. S. (2014). Red Skin, White Masks: Rejecting the Colonial Politics of Recognition. University of Minnesota Press.

6. Cunneen, C., & Tauri, J. M. (2016). Indigenous Criminology. Policy Press.

7. Hart, M. A. (2002). Seeking Mino-Pimatisiwin: An Aboriginal Approach to Healing. Fernwood Publishing.

8. Johnston, B. (1988). Ojibway Heritage. University of Nebraska Press.

9. Justice, D. H. (2008). Our Fire Survives the Storm: A Cherokee Literary History. University of Minnesota Press.

10. LaRocque, E. (2010). When the Other is Me: Native Resistance Discourse, 1850-1990. University of Manitoba Press.

11. McCaslin, W. D., & Boyer, Y. (2009). First Nations Communities at Risk and in Crisis: Justice and Security. Aboriginal Healing Foundation.

12. Ross, R. (1996). Returning to the Teachings: Exploring Aboriginal Justice. Penguin Random House Canada.

13. Sinclair, M., Littlechild, W., & Wilson, M. (2015). The Final Report of the Truth and Reconciliation Commission of Canada. McGill-Queen's University Press.

14. Smith, L. T. (2012). Decolonizing Methodologies: Research and Indigenous Peoples. Zed Books.

15. Taiaiake, A., & Corntassel, J. (2005). Being Indigenous: Resurgences Against Contemporary Colonialism. Government and Opposition, 40(4), 597-614.

16. Tauri, J. M., & Morris, A. (1997). Reform or Resistance? Restorative Justice in New Zealand and Indigenous Critique. The British Journal of Criminology, 37(2), 481-502.

17. Truth and Reconciliation Commission of Canada. (2015). Honouring the Truth, Reconciling for the Future: Summary of the Final Report of the Truth and Reconciliation Commission of Canada. Government of Canada.

18. Waldram, J. B. (2008). Revenge of the Windigo: The Construction of the Mind and Mental Health of North American Aboriginal Peoples. University of Toronto Press.

This list provides a diverse range of works that discuss Indigenous justice systems, the principles of restorative justice, and the broader context of reconciliation. These sources include foundational academic works, government reports, and writings from Indigenous scholars and practitioners.